CLEP-9   COLLEGE-LEVEL EXAMINATION
         PROGRAM SERIES

This is your
PASSBOOK for...

Introduction to Educational Psychology

Test Preparation Study Guide
Questions & Answers

NATIONAL LEARNING CORPORATION ®

COPYRIGHT NOTICE

This book is SOLELY intended for, is sold ONLY to, and its use is RESTRICTED to individual, bona fide applicants or candidates who qualify by virtue of having seriously filed applications for appropriate license, certificate, professional and/or promotional advancement, higher school matriculation, scholarship, or other legitimate requirements of education and/or governmental authorities.

This book is NOT intended for use, class instruction, tutoring, training, duplication, copying, reprinting, excerption, or adaptation, etc., by:

1) Other publishers
2) Proprietors and/or Instructors of "Coaching" and/or Preparatory Courses
3) Personnel and/or Training Divisions of commercial, industrial, and governmental organizations
4) Schools, colleges, or universities and/or their departments and staffs, including teachers and other personnel
5) Testing Agencies or Bureaus
6) Study groups which seek by the purchase of a single volume to copy and/or duplicate and/or adapt this material for use by the group as a whole without having purchased individual volumes for each of the members of the group
7) Et al.

Such persons would be in violation of appropriate Federal and State statutes.

PROVISION OF LICENSING AGREEMENTS – Recognized educational, commercial, industrial, and governmental institutions and organizations, and others legitimately engaged in educational pursuits, including training, testing, and measurement activities, may address request for a licensing agreement to the copyright owners, who will determine whether, and under what conditions, including fees and charges, the materials in this book may be used them. In other words, a licensing facility exists for the legitimate use of the material in this book on other than an individual basis. However, it is asseverated and affirmed here that the material in this book CANNOT be used without the receipt of the express permission of such a licensing agreement from the Publishers. Inquiries re licensing should be addressed to the company, attention rights and permissions department.

All rights reserved, including the right of reproduction in whole or in part, in any form or by any means, electronic or mechanical, including photocopying, recording, or by any information storage and retrieval system, without permission in writing from the Publisher.

Copyright © 2025 by
National Learning Corporation

212 Michael Drive, Syosset, NY 11791
(516) 921-8888 • www.passbooks.com
E-mail: info@passbooks.com

PASSBOOK® SERIES

THE *PASSBOOK® SERIES* has been created to prepare applicants and candidates for the ultimate academic battlefield – the examination room.

At some time in our lives, each and every one of us may be required to take an examination – for validation, matriculation, admission, qualification, registration, certification, or licensure.

Based on the assumption that every applicant or candidate has met the basic formal educational standards, has taken the required number of courses, and read the necessary texts, the *PASSBOOK® SERIES* furnishes the one special preparation which may assure passing with confidence, instead of failing with insecurity. Examination questions – together with answers – are furnished as the basic vehicle for study so that the mysteries of the examination and its compounding difficulties may be eliminated or diminished by a sure method.

This book is meant to help you pass your examination provided that you qualify and are serious in your objective.

The entire field is reviewed through the huge store of content information which is succinctly presented through a provocative and challenging approach – the question-and-answer method.

A climate of success is established by furnishing the correct answers at the end of each test.

You soon learn to recognize types of questions, forms of questions, and patterns of questioning. You may even begin to anticipate expected outcomes.

You perceive that many questions are repeated or adapted so that you can gain acute insights, which may enable you to score many sure points.

You learn how to confront new questions, or types of questions, and to attack them confidently and work out the correct answers.

You note objectives and emphases, and recognize pitfalls and dangers, so that you may make positive educational adjustments.

Moreover, you are kept fully informed in relation to new concepts, methods, practices, and directions in the field.

You discover that you are actually taking the examination all the time: you are preparing for the examination by "taking" an examination, not by reading extraneous and/or supererogatory textbooks.

In short, this PASSBOOK®, used directedly, should be an important factor in helping you to pass your test.

NONTRADITIONAL EDUCATION

Students returning to school as adults bring more varied experience to their studies than do the teenagers who begin college shortly after graduating from high school. As a result, there are numerous programs for students with nontraditional learning curves. Hundreds of colleges and universities grant degrees to people who cannot attend classes at a regular campus or have already learned what the college is supposed to teach.

You can earn nontraditional education credits in many ways:
- Passing standardized exams
- Demonstrating knowledge gained through experience
- Completing campus-based coursework, and
- Taking courses off campus

Some methods of assessing learning for credit are objective, such as standardized tests. Others are more subjective, such as a review of life experiences.

With some help from four hypothetical characters – Alice, Vin, Lynette, and Jorge – this article describes nontraditional ways of earning educational credit. It begins by describing programs in which you can earn a high school diploma without spending 4 years in a classroom. The college picture is more complicated, so it is presented in two parts: one on gaining credit for what you know through course work or experience, and a second on college degree programs. The final section lists resources for locating more information.

Earning High School Credit

People who were prevented from finishing high school as teenagers have several options if they want to do so as adults. Some major cities have back-to-school programs that allow adults to attend high school classes with current students. But the more practical alternatives for most adults are to take the General Educational Development (GED) tests or to earn a high school diploma by demonstrating their skills or taking correspondence classes.

Of course, these options do not match the experience of staying in high school and graduating with one's friends. But they are viable alternatives for adult learners committed to meeting and, often, continuing their educational goals.

GED Program

Alice quit high school her sophomore year and took a job to help support herself, her younger brother, and their newly widowed mother. Now an adult, she wants to earn her high school diploma – and then go on to college. Because her job as head cook and her family responsibilities keep her busy during the day, she plans to get a high school equivalency diploma. She will study for, and take, the GED tests. Every year, about half a million adults earn their high school credentials this way. A GED diploma is accepted in lieu of a high school one by more than 90 percent of employers, colleges, and universities, so it is a good choice for someone like Alice.

The GED testing program is sponsored by the American Council on Education and State and local education departments. It consists of examinations in five subject areas: Writing, science, mathematics, social studies, and literature and the arts. The tests also measure skills such as analytical ability, problem solving, reading comprehension, and ability to understand and apply information. Most of the questions are multiple choice; the writing test includes an essay section on a topic of general interest.

Eligibility rules for taking the exams vary, but some states require that you must be at least 18. Tests are given in English, Spanish, and French. In addition to standard print, versions in large print, Braille, and audiocassette are also available. Total time allotted for the tests is 7 1/2 hours.

The GED tests are not easy. About one-fourth of those who complete the exams every year do not pass. Passing scores are established by administering the tests to a sample of graduating high school seniors. The minimum standard score is set so that about one-third of graduating seniors would not pass the tests if they took them.

Because of the difficulty of the tests, people need to prepare themselves to take them. Often, they start by taking the Official GED Practice Tests, usually available through a local adult education center. Centers are listed in your phone book's blue pages under "Adult Education," "Continuing Education," or "GED." Adult education centers also have information about GED preparation classes and self-study materials. Classes are generally arranged to accommodate adults' work schedules. National Learning Corporation publishes several study guides that aim to thoroughly prepare test-takers for the GED.

School districts, colleges, adult education centers, and community organizations have information about GED testing schedules and practice tests. For more information, contact them, your nearest GED testing center, or:
GED Testing Service
One Dupont Circle, NW, Suite 250
Washington, DC 20036-1163
1(800) 62-MY GED (626-9433)
(202) 939-9490

Skills Demonstration

Adults who have acquired high school level skills through experience might be eligible for the National External Diploma Program. This alternative to the GED does not involve any direct instruction. Instead, adults seeking a high school diploma must demonstrate mastery of 65 competencies in 8 general areas: Communication; computation; occupational preparedness; and self, social, consumer, scientific, and technological awareness.

Mastery is shown through the completion of the tasks. For example, a participant could prove competency in computation by measuring a room for carpeting, figuring out the amount of carpet needed, and computing the cost.

Before being accepted for the program, adults undergo an evaluation. Tests taken at one of the program's offices measure reading, writing, and mathematics abilities. A take-home segment includes a self-assessment of current skills, an individual skill evaluation, and an occupational interest and aptitude test.

Adults accepted for the program have weekly meetings with an assessor. At the meeting, the assessor reviews the participant's work from the previous week. If the task has not been completed properly, the assessor explains the mistake. Participants continue to correct their errors until they master each competency. A high school diploma is awarded upon proven mastery of all 65 competencies.

Fourteen States and the District of Columbia now offer the External Diploma Program. For more information, contact:
External Diploma Program
One Dupont Circle, NW, Suite 250
Washington, DC 20036-1193
(202) 939-9475

Correspondence and Distance Study
Vin dropped out of high school during his junior year because his family's frequent moves made it difficult for him to continue his studies. He promised himself at the time he dropped out that he would someday finish the courses needed for his diploma. For people like Vin, who prefer to earn a traditional diploma in a nontraditional way, there are about a dozen accredited courses of study for earning a high school diploma by correspondence, or distance study. The programs are either privately run, affiliated with a university, or administered by a State education department.

Distance study diploma programs have no residency requirements, allowing students to continue their studies from almost any location. Depending on the course of study, students need not be enrolled full time and usually have more flexible schedules for finishing their work. Selection of courses ranges from vo-tech to college prep, and some programs place different emphasis on the types of diplomas offered. University affiliated schools, for example, allow qualified students to take college courses along with their high school ones. Students can then apply the college credits toward a degree at that university or transfer them to another institution.

Taking courses by distance study is often more challenging and time consuming than attending classes, especially for adults who have other obligations. Success depends on each student's motivation. Students usually do reading assignments on their own. Written exercises, which they complete and send to an instructor for grading, supplement their reading material.

A list of some accredited high schools that offer diplomas by distance study is available free from the Distance Education and Training Council, formerly known as the National Home Study Council. Request the "DETC Directory of Accredited Institutions" from:
The Distance Education and Training Council
1601 18th Street, NW.
Washington, DC 20009-2529
(202) 234-5100

Some publications profiling nontraditional college programs include addresses and descriptions of several high school correspondence ones. See the Resources section at the end of this article for more information.

Getting College Credit For What You Know
Adults can receive college credit for prior coursework, by passing examinations, and documenting experiential learning. With help from a college advisor, nontraditional students should assess their skills, establish their educational goals, and determine the number of college credits they might be eligible for.

Even before you meet with a college advisor, you should collect all your school and training records. Then, make a list of all knowledge and abilities acquired through experience, no matter how irrelevant they seem to your chosen field. Next, determine your educational goals: What specific field do you wish to study? What kind of a degree do you want? Finally, determine how your past work fits into the field of study. Later on, you will evaluate educational programs to find one that's right for you.

People who have complex educational or experiential learning histories might want to have their learning evaluated by the Regents Credit Bank. The Credit Bank, operated by Regents College of the University of the State of New York, allows people to consolidate credits earned through college, experience, or other methods. Special assessments are available for Regents College enrollees whose knowledge in a specific field cannot be adequately evaluated by standardized exams. For more information, contact the Regents Credit Bank at:

Regents College
7 Columbia Circle
Albany, NY 12203-5159
(518) 464-8500

Credit For Prior College Coursework

When Lynette was in college during the 1970s, she attended several different schools and took a variety of courses. She did well in some classes and poorly in others. Now that she is a successful business owner and has more focus, Lynette thinks she should forget about her previous coursework and start from scratch. Instead, she should start from where she is.

Lynette should have all her transcripts sent to the colleges or universities of her choice and let an admissions officer determine which classes are applicable toward a degree. A few credits here and there may not seem like much, but they add up. Even if the subjects do not seem relevant to any major, they might be counted as elective credits toward a degree. And comparing the cost of transcripts with the cost of college courses, it makes sense to spend a few dollars per transcript for a chance to save hundreds, and perhaps thousands, of dollars in books and tuition.

Rules for transferring credits apply to all prior coursework at accredited colleges and universities, whether done on campus or off. Courses completed off campus, often called extended learning, include those available to students through independent study and correspondence. Many schools have extended learning programs; Brigham Young University, for example, offers more than 300 courses through its Department of Independent Study. One type of extended learning is distance learning, a form of correspondence study by technological means such as television, video and audio, CD-ROM, electronic mail, and computer tutorials. See the Resources section at the end of this article for more information about publications available from the National University Continuing Education Association.

Any previously earned college credits should be considered for transfer, no matter what the subject or the grade received. Many schools do not accept the transfer of courses graded below a C or ones taken more than a designated number of years ago. Some colleges and universities also have limits on the number of credits that can be transferred and applied toward a degree. But not all do. For example, Thomas Edison State College, New Jersey's State college for adults, accepts the transfer of all 120 hours of credit required for a baccalaureate degree – provided all the credits are transferred from regionally accredited schools, no more than 80 are at the junior college level, and the student's grades overall and in the field of study average out to C.

To assign credit for prior coursework, most schools require original transcripts. This means you must complete a form or send a written, signed request to have your transcripts released directly to a college or university. Once you have chosen the schools you want to apply to, contact the schools you attended before. Find out how much each transcript costs, and ask them to send your transcripts to the ones you are applying to. Write a letter that includes your name (and names used during attendance, if different) and dates of attendance, along with the names and addresses of the schools to which your transcripts should be sent. Include payment and mail to the registrar at the schools you have attended. The registrar's office will process your request and send an official transcript of your coursework to the colleges or universities you have designated.

Credit For Noncollege Courses

Colleges and universities are not the only ones that offer classes. Volunteer organizations and employers often provide formal training worth college credit. The American Council on Education has two programs that assess thousands of specific courses and make recommendations on the amount of college credit they are worth. Colleges and universities accept the recommendations or use them as guidelines.

One program evaluates educational courses sponsored by government agencies, business and industry, labor unions, and professional and voluntary organizations. It is the Program on Noncollegiate Sponsored Instruction (PONSI). Some of the training seminars Alice has participated in covered topics such as food preparation, kitchen safety, and nutrition. Although she has not yet earned her GED, Alice can earn college credit because of her completion of these formal job-training seminars. The number of credits each seminar is worth does not hinge on Alice's current eligibility for college enrollment.

The other program evaluates courses offered by the Army, Navy, Air Force, Marines, Coast Guard, and Department of Defense. It is the Military Evaluations Program. Jorge has never attended college, but the engineering technology classes he completed as part of his military training are worth college credit. And as an Army veteran, Jorge is eligible for a service that takes the evaluations one step further. The Army/American Council on Education Registry Transcript System (AARTS) will provide Jorge with an individualized transcript of American Council on Education credit recommendations for all courses he completed, the military occupational specialties (MOS's) he held, and examinations he passed while in the Army. All Army and National Guard enlisted personnel and veterans who enlisted after October 1981 are eligible for the transcript. Similar services are being considered by the Navy and Marine Corps.

To obtain a free transcript, see your Army Education Center for a 5454R transcript request form. Include your name, Social Security number, basic active service date, and complete address where you want the transcript sent. Mail your request to:

AARTS Operations Center
415 McPherson Ave.
Fort Leavenworth, KS 66027-1373

Recommendations for PONSI are published in *The National Guide to Educational Credit for Training Programs;* military program recommendations are in *The Guide to the Evaluation of Educational Experiences in the Armed Forces.* See the Resources section at the end of this article for more information about these publications.

Former military personnel who took a foreign language course through the Defense Language Institute may request course transcripts by sending their name, Social Security number, course title, duration of the course, and graduation date to:

    Commandant, Defense Language Institute
    Attn: ATFL-DAA-AR
    Transcripts
    Presidio of Monterey
    Monterey, CA 93944-5006

Not all of Jorge's and Alice's courses have been assessed by the American Council on Education. Training courses that have no Council credit recommendation should still be assessed by an advisor at the schools they want to attend. Course descriptions, class notes, test scores, and other documentation may be helpful for comparing training courses to their college equivalents. An oral examination or other demonstration of competency might also be required.

There is no guarantee you will receive all the credits you are seeking – but you certainly won't if you make no attempt.

Credit By Examination

Standardized tests are the best-known method of receiving college credit without taking courses. These exams are often taken by high school students seeking advanced placement for college, but they are also available to adult learners. Testing programs and colleges and universities offer exams in a number of subjects. Two U.S. Government institutes have foreign language exams for employees that also may be worth college credit.

It is important to understand that receiving a passing score on these exams does not mean you get college credit automatically. Each school determines which test results it will accept, minimum scores required, how scores are converted for credit, and the amount of credit, if any, to be assigned. Most colleges and universities accept the American Council on Education credit recommendations, published every other year in the 250-page *Guide to Educational Credit by Examination*. For more information, contact:

    The American Council on Education
    Credit by Examination Program
    One Dupont Circle, Suite 250
    Washington, DC 20036-1193
    (202) 939-9434

Testing programs:

You might know some of the five national testing programs by their acronyms or initials: CLEP, ACT PEP: RCE, DANTES, AP, and NOCTI. (The meanings of these initialisms are explained below.) There is some overlap among programs; for example, four of them have introductory accounting exams. Since you will not be awarded credit more than once for a specific subject, you should carefully evaluate each program for the subject exams you wish to take. And before taking an exam, make sure you will be awarded credit by the college or university you plan to attend.

CLEP (College-Level Examination Program), administered by the College Board, is the most widely accepted of the national testing programs; more than 2,800 accredited schools award credit for passing exam scores. Each test covers material taught in basic

undergraduate courses. There are five general exams – English composition, humanities, college mathematics, natural sciences, and social sciences and history – and many subject exams. Most exams are entirely multiple-choice, but English composition exams may include an essay section. For more information, contact:
> CLEP
> P.O. Box 6600
> Princeton, NJ 08541-6600
> (609) 771-7865

ACT PEP: RCE (American College Testing Proficiency Exam Program: Regents College Examinations) tests are given in 38 subjects within arts and sciences, business, education, and nursing. Each exam is recommended for either lower- or upper-level credit. Exams contain either objective or extended response questions, and are graded according to a standard score, letter grade, or pass/fail. Fees vary, depending on the subject and type of exam. For more information or to request free study guides, contact:
> ACT PEP: Regents College Examinations
> P.O. Box 4014
> Iowa City, IA 52243
> (319) 337-1387
> (New York State residents must contact Regents College directly.)

DANTES (Defense Activity for Nontraditional Education Support) standardized tests are developed by the Educational Testing Service for the Department of Defense. Originally administered only to military personnel, the exams have been available to the public since 1983. About 50 subject tests cover business, mathematics, social science, physical science, humanities, foreign languages, and applied technology. Most of the tests consist entirely of multiple-choice questions. Schools determine their own administering fees and testing schedules. For more information or to request free study sheets, contact:
> DANTES Program Office
> Mail Stop 31-X
> Educational Testing Service
> Princeton, NJ 08541
> 1(800) 257-9484

The AP (Advanced Placement) Program is a cooperative effort between secondary schools and colleges and universities. AP exams are developed each year by committees of college and high school faculty appointed by the College Board and assisted by consultants from the Educational Testing Service. Subjects include arts and languages, natural sciences, computer science, social sciences, history, and mathematics. Most tests are 2 or 3 hours long and include both multiple-choice and essay questions. AP courses are available to help students prepare for exams, which are offered in the spring. For more information about the Advanced Placement Program, contact:
> Advanced Placement Services
> P.O. Box 6671
> Princeton, NJ 08541-6671
> (609) 771-7300

NOCTI (National Occupational Competency Testing Institute) assessments are designed for people like Alice, who have vocational-technical skills that cannot be evaluated by other tests. NOCTI assesses competency at two levels: Student/job ready and teacher/experienced worker. Standardized evaluations are available for occupations such as auto-body repair, electronics, mechanical drafting, quantity food preparation, and upholstering. The tests consist of multiple-choice questions and a performance component. Other services include workshops, customized assessments, and pre-testing. For more information, contact:

NOCTI
500 N. Bronson Ave.
Ferris State University
Big Rapids, MI 49307
(616) 796-4699

Colleges and universities:

Many colleges and universities have credit-by-exam programs, through which students earn credit by passing a comprehensive exam for a course offered by the institution. Among the most widely recognized are the programs at Ohio University, the University of North Carolina, Thomas Edison State College, and New York University.

Ohio University offers about 150 examinations for credit. In addition, you may sometimes arrange to take special examinations in non-laboratory courses offered at Ohio University. To take a test for credit, you must enroll in the course. If you plan to transfer the credit earned, you also need written permission from an official at your school. Books and study materials are available, for a cost, through the university. Exams must be taken within 6 months of the enrollment date; most last 3 hours. You may arrange to take the exam off campus if you do not live near the university.

Ohio University is on the quarter-hour system; most courses are worth 4 quarter hours, the equivalent of 3 semester hours. For more information, contact:

Independent Study
Tupper Hall 302
Ohio University
Athens, OH 45701-2979
1(800) 444-2910
(614) 593-2910

The University of North Carolina offers a credit-by-examination option for 140 independent study (correspondence) courses in foreign languages, humanities, social sciences, mathematics, business administration, education, electrical and computer engineering, health administration, and natural sciences. To take an exam, you must request and receive approval from both the course instructor and the independent studies department. Exams must be taken within six months of enrollment, and you may register for no more than two at a time. If you are not near the University's Chapel Hill campus, you may take your exam under supervision at an accredited college, university, community college, or technical institute. For more information, contact:

Independent Studies
CB #1020, The Friday Center
UNC-Chapel Hill
Chapel Hill, NC 27599-1020
1(800) 862-5669 / (919) 962-1134

The Thomas Edison College Examination Program offers more than 50 exams in liberal arts, business, and professional areas. Thomas Edison State College administers tests twice a month in Trenton, New Jersey; however, students may arrange to take their tests with a proctor at any accredited American college or university or U.S. military base. Most of the tests are multiple choice; some also include short answer or essay questions. Time limits range from 90 minutes to 4 hours, depending on the exam. For more information, contact:

Thomas Edison State College
TECEP, Office of Testing and Assessment
101 W. State Street
Trenton, NJ 08608-1176
(609) 633-2844

New York University's Foreign Language Program offers proficiency exams in more than 40 languages, from Albanian to Yiddish. Two exams are available in each language: The 12-point test is equivalent to 4 undergraduate semesters, and the 16-point exam may lead to upper level credit. The tests are given at the university's Foreign Language Department throughout the year.

Proof of foreign language proficiency does not guarantee college credit. Some colleges and universities accept transcripts only for languages commonly taught, such as French and Spanish. Nontraditional programs are more likely than traditional ones to grant credit for proficiency in other languages.

For an informational brochure and registration form for NYU's foreign language proficiency exams, contact:

New York University
Foreign Language Department
48 Cooper Square, Room 107
New York, NY 10003
(212) 998-7030

Government institutes:

The Defense Language Institute and Foreign Service Institute administer foreign language proficiency exams for personnel stationed abroad. Usually, the tests are given at the end of intensive language courses or upon completion of service overseas. But some people – like Jorge, who knows Spanish – speak another language fluently and may be allowed to take a proficiency exam in that language before completing their tour of duty. Contact one of the offices listed below to obtain transcripts of those scores. Proof of proficiency does not guarantee college credit, however, as discussed above.

To request score reports from the Defense Language Institute for Defense Language Proficiency Tests, send your name, Social Security number, language for which you were tested, and, most importantly, when and where you took the exam to:

Commandant, Defense Language Institute
Attn: ATFL-ES-T
DLPT Score Report Request
Presidio of Monterey
Monterey, CA 93944-5006

To request transcripts of scores for Foreign Service Institute exams, send your name, Social Security number, language for which you were tested, and dates or year of exams to:

Foreign Service Institute
Arlington Hall
4020 Arlington Boulevard
Rosslyn, VA 22204-1500
Attn: Testing Office (Send your request to the attention of the testing office of the foreign language in which you were tested)

Credit For Experience

Experiential learning credit may be given for knowledge gained through job responsibilities, personal hobbies, volunteer opportunities, homemaking, and other experiences. Colleges and universities base credit awards on the knowledge you have attained, not for the experience alone. In addition, the knowledge must be college level; not just any learning will do. Throwing horseshoes as a hobby is not likely to be worth college credit. But if you've done research on how and where the sport originated, visited blacksmiths, organized tournaments, and written a column for a trade journal — well, that's a horseshoe of a different color.

Adults attempting to get credit for their experience should be forewarned: Having your experience evaluated for college credit is time-consuming, tedious work — not an easy shortcut for people who want quick-fix college credits. And not all experience, no matter how valuable, is the equivalent of college courses.

Requesting college credit for your experiential learning can be tricky. You should get assistance from a credit evaluations officer at the school you plan to attend, but you should also have a general idea of what your knowledge is worth. A common method for converting knowledge into credit is to use a college catalog. Find course titles and descriptions that match what you have learned through experience, and request the number of credits offered for those courses.

Once you know what credit to ask for, you must usually present your case in writing to officials at the college you plan to attend. The most common form of presenting experiential learning for credit is the portfolio. A portfolio is a written record of your knowledge along with a request for equivalent college credit. It includes an identification and description of the knowledge for which you are requesting credit, an explanatory essay of how the knowledge was gained and how it fits into your educational plans, documentation that you have acquired such knowledge, and a request for college credit. Required elements of a portfolio vary by schools but generally follow those guidelines.

In identifying knowledge you have gained, be specific about exactly what you have learned. For example, it is not enough for Lynette to say she runs a business. She must identify the knowledge she has gained from running it, such as personnel management, tax law, marketing strategy, and inventory review. She must also include brief descriptions about her knowledge of each to support her claims of having those skills.

The essay gives you a chance to relay something about who you are. It should address your educational goals, include relevant autobiographical details, and be well organized, neat, and convey confidence. In his essay, Jorge might first state his goal of becoming an engineer. Then he would explain why he joined the Army, where he got hands-on training and experience in developing and servicing electronic equipment.

This, he would say, led to his hobby of creating remote-controlled model cars, of which he has built 20. His conclusion would highlight his accomplishments and tie them to his desire to become an electronic engineer.

Documentation is evidence that you've learned what you claim to have learned. You can show proof of knowledge in a variety of ways, including audio or video recordings, letters from current or former employers describing your specific duties and job performance, blueprints, photographs or artwork, and transcripts of certifying exams for professional licenses and certification – such as Alice's certification from the American Culinary Federation. Although documentation can take many forms, written proof alone is not always enough. If it is impossible to document your knowledge in writing, find out if your experiential learning can be assessed through supplemental oral exams by a faculty expert.

Earning a College Degree

Nontraditional students often have work, family, and financial obligations that prevent them from quitting their jobs to attend school full time. Can they still meet their educational goals? Yes.

More than 150 accredited colleges and universities have nontraditional bachelor's degree programs that require students to spend little or no time on campus; over 300 others have nontraditional campus-based degree programs. Some of those schools, as well as most junior and community colleges, offer associate's degrees nontraditionally. Each school with a nontraditional course of study determines its own rules for awarding credit for prior coursework, exams, or experience, as discussed previously. Most have charges on top of tuition for providing these special services.

Several publications profile nontraditional degree programs; see the Resources section at the end of this article for more information. To determine which school best fits your academic profile and educational goals, first list your criteria. Then, evaluate nontraditional programs based on their accreditation, features, residency requirements, and expenses. Once you have chosen several schools to explore further, write to them for more information. Detailed explanations of school policies should help you decide which ones you want to apply to.

Get beyond the printed word – especially the glowing words each school writes about itself. Check out the schools you are considering with higher education authorities, alumni, employers, family members, and friends. If possible, visit the campus to talk to students and instructors and sit in on a few classes, even if you will be completing most or all of your work off campus. Ask school officials questions about such things as enrollment numbers, graduation rate, faculty qualifications, and confusing details about the application process or academic policies. After you have thoroughly investigated each prospective college or university, you can make an informed decision about which is right for you.

Accreditation

Accreditation is a process colleges and universities submit to voluntarily for getting their credentials. An accredited school has been investigated and visited by teams of observers and has periodic inspections by a private accrediting agency. The initial review can take two years or more.

Regional agencies accredit entire schools, and professional agencies accredit either specialized schools or departments within schools. Although there are no national accrediting standards, not just any accreditation will do. Countless "accreditation associations" have been invented by schools, many of which have no academic programs and sell phony degrees, to accredit themselves. But 6 regional and about 80 professional accrediting associations in the United States are recognized by the U.S. Department of Education or the Commission on Recognition of Postsecondary Accreditation. When checking accreditation, these are the names to look for. For more information about accreditation and accrediting agencies, contact:

    Institutional Participation Oversight Service Accreditation and State Liaison Division
    U.S. Department of Education
    ROB 3, Room 3915
    600 Independence Ave., SW
    Washington, DC 20202-5244
    (202) 708-7417

Because accreditation is not mandatory, lack of accreditation does not necessarily mean a school or program is bad. Some schools choose not to apply for accreditation, are in the process of applying, or have educational methods too unconventional for an accrediting association's standards. For the nontraditional student, however, earning a degree from a college or university with recognized accreditation is an especially important consideration. Although nontraditional education is becoming more widely accepted, it is not yet mainstream. Employers skeptical of a degree earned in a nontraditional manner are likely to be even less accepting of one from an unaccredited school.

Program Features

Because nontraditional students have diverse educational objectives, nontraditional schools are diverse in what they offer. Some programs are geared toward helping students organize their scattered educational credits to get a degree as quickly as possible. Others cater to those who may have specific credits or experience but need assistance in completing requirements. Whatever your educational profile, you should look for a program that works with you in obtaining your educational goals.

A few nontraditional programs have special admissions policies for adult learners like Alice, who plan to earn their GEDs but want to enroll in college in the meantime. Other features of nontraditional programs include individualized learning agreements, intensive academic counseling, cooperative learning and internship placement, and waiver of some prerequisites or other requirements – as well as college credit for prior coursework, examinations, and experiential learning, all discussed previously.

Lynette, whose primary goal is to finish her degree, wants to earn maximum credits for her business experience. She will look for programs that do not limit the number of credits awarded for equivalency exams and experiential learning. And since well-documented proof of knowledge is essential for earning experiential learning credits, Lynette should make sure the program she chooses provides assistance to students submitting a portfolio.

Jorge, on the other hand, has more credits than he needs in certain areas and is willing to forego some. To become an engineer, he must have a bachelor's degree; but because he is accustomed to hands-on learning, Jorge is interested in getting experience as he gains more technical skills. He will concentrate on finding schools with strong cooperative education, supervised fieldwork, or internship programs.

Residency Requirements

Programs are sometimes deemed nontraditional because of their residency requirements. Many people think of residency for colleges and universities in terms of tuition, with in-state students paying less than out-of-state ones. Residency also may refer to where a student lives, either on or off campus, while attending school.

But in nontraditional education, residency usually refers to how much time students must spend on campus, regardless of whether they attend classes there. In some nontraditional programs, students need not ever step foot on campus. Others require only a very short residency, such as one day or a few weeks. Many schools have standard residency requirements of several semesters but schedule classes for evenings or weekends to accommodate working adults.

Lynette, who previously took courses by independent study, prefers to earn credits by distance study. She will focus on schools that have no residency requirement. Several colleges and universities have nonresident degree completion programs for adults with some college credit. Under the direction of a faculty advisor, students devise a plan for earning their remaining credits. Methods for earning credits include independent study, distance learning, seminars, supervised fieldwork, and group study at arranged sites. Students may have to earn a certain number of credits through the degree-granting institution. But many programs allow students to take courses at accredited schools of their choice for transfer toward their degree.

Alice wants to attend lectures but has an unpredictable schedule. Her best course of action will be to seek out short residency programs that require students to attend seminars once or twice a semester. She can take courses that are televised and videotape them to watch when her schedule permits, with the seminars helping to ensure that she properly completes her coursework. Many colleges and universities with short residency requirements also permit students to earn some credits elsewhere, by whatever means the student chooses.

Some fields of study require classroom instruction. As Jorge will discover, few colleges and universities allow students to earn a bachelor's degree in engineering entirely through independent study. Nontraditional residency programs are designed to accommodate adults' daytime work schedules. Jorge should look for programs offering evening, weekend, summer, and accelerated courses.

Tuition and Other Expenses

The final decisions about which schools Alice, Jorge, and Lynette attend may hinge in large part on a single issue: Cost. And rising tuition is only part of the equation. Beginning with application fees and continuing through graduation fees, college expenses add up.

Traditional and nontraditional students have some expenses in common, such as the cost of books and other materials. Tuition might even be the same for some courses, especially for colleges and universities offering standard ones at unusual times. But for nontraditional programs, students may also pay fees for services such as credit or transcript review, evaluation, advisement, and portfolio assessment.

Students are also responsible for postage and handling or setup expenses for independent study courses, as well as for all examination and transcript fees for transferring credits. Usually, the more nontraditional the program, the more detailed the fees. Some schools charge a yearly enrollment fee rather than tuition for degree completion candidates who want their files to remain active.

Although tuition and fees might seem expensive, most educators tell you not to let money come between you and your educational goals. Talk to someone in the financial aid department of the school you plan to attend or check your library for publications about financial aid sources. The U.S. Department of Education publishes a guide to Federal aid programs such as Pell Grants, student loans, and work-study. To order the free 74-page booklet, *The Student Guide: Financial Aid from the U.S. Department of Education,* contact:

Federal Student Aid Information Center
P.O. Box 84
Washington, DC 20044
1 (800) 4FED-AID (433-3243)

Resources

Information on how to earn a high school diploma or college degree without following the usual routes is available from several organizations and in numerous publications. Information on nontraditional graduate degree programs, available for master's through doctoral level, though not discussed in this article, can usually be obtained from the same resources that detail bachelor's degree programs.

National Learning Corporation publishes study guides for all of these exams, for both general examinations and tests in specific subject areas. To order study guides, or to browse their catalog featuring more than 5,000 titles, visit NLC online at www.passbooks.com, or contact them by phone at (800) 632-8888.

Organizations

Adult learners should always contact their local school system, community college, or university to learn about programs that are readily available. The following national organizations can also supply information:

American Council on Education
One Dupont Circle
Washington, DC 20036-1193
(202) 939-9300

Within the American Council on Education, the Center for Adult Learning and Educational Credentials administers the National External Diploma Program, the GED Program, the Program on Noncollegiate Sponsored Instruction, the Credit by Examination Program, and the Military Evaluations Program.

College-Level Examination Program (CLEP)

1. WHAT IS CLEP?

CLEP stands for the College-Level Examination Program, sponsored by the College Board. It is a national program of credit-by-examination that offers you the opportunity to obtain recognition for college-level achievement. No matter when, where, or how you have learned – by means of formal or informal study – you can take CLEP tests. If the results are acceptable to your college, you can receive credit.

You may not realize it, but you probably know more than your academic record reveals. Each day you, like most people, have an opportunity to learn. In private industry and business, as well as at all levels of government, learning opportunities continually occur. If you read widely or intensively in a particular field, think about what you read, discuss it with your family and friends, you are learning. Or you may be learning on a more formal basis by taking a correspondence course, a television or radio course, a course recorded on tape or cassettes, a course assembled into programmed tests, or a course taught in your community adult school or high school.

No matter how, where, or when you gained your knowledge, you may have the opportunity to receive academic credit for your achievement that can be counted toward an undergraduate degree. The College-Level Examination Program (CLEP) enables colleges to evaluate your achievement and give you credit. A wide range of college-level examinations are offered by CLEP to anyone who wishes to take them. Scores on the tests are reported to you and, if you wish, to a college, employer, or individual.

2. WHAT ARE THE PURPOSES OF THE COLLEGE-LEVEL EXAMINATION PROGRAM?

The basic purpose of the College-Level Examination Program is to enable individuals who have acquired their education in nontraditional ways to demonstrate their academic achievement. It is also intended for use by those in higher education, business, industry, government, and other fields who need a reliable method of assessing a person's educational level.

Recognizing that the real issue is not how a person has acquired his education but what education he has, the College Level Examination Program has been designed to serve a variety of purposes. The basic purpose, as listed above, is to enable those who have reached the college level of education in nontraditional ways to assess the level of their achievement and to use the test results in seeking college credit or placement.

In addition, scores on the tests can be used to validate educational experience obtained at a nonaccredited institution or through noncredit college courses.

Some colleges and universities may use the tests to measure the level of educational achievement of their students, and for various institutional research purposes.

Other colleges and universities may wish to use the tests in the admission, placement, and guidance of students who wish to transfer from one institution to another.

Businesses, industries, governmental agencies, and professional groups now accept the results of these tests as a basis for advancement, eligibility for further training, or professional or semi-professional certification.

Many people are interested in the examination simply to assess their own educational progress and attainment.

The college, university, business, industry, or government agency that adopts the tests in the College-Level Examination Program makes its own decision about how it will use and interpret the test scores. The College Board will provide the tests, score them, and report the results either to the individuals who took the tests or the college or agency that administered them. It does NOT, and cannot, award college credit, certify college equivalency, or make recommendations regarding the standards these institutions should establish for the use of the test results.

Therefore, if you are taking the tests to secure credit from an institution, you should FIRST ascertain whether the college or agency involved will accept the scores. Each institution determines which CLEP tests it will accept for credit and the amount of credit it will award. If you want to take tests for college credit, first call, write, or visit the college you wish to attend to inquire about its policy on CLEP scores, as well as its other admission requirements.

The services of the program are also available to people who have been requested to take the tests by an employer, a professional licensing agency, a certifying agency, or by other groups that recognize college equivalency on the basis of satisfactory CLEP scores. You may, of course, take the tests SOLELY for your own information. If you do, your scores will be reported only to you.

While neither CLEP nor the College Board can evaluate previous credentials or award college credit, you will receive, with your scores, basic information to help you interpret your performance on the tests you have taken.

3. WHAT ARE THE COLLEGE-LEVEL EXAMINATIONS?

In order to meet different kinds of curricular organization and testing needs at colleges and universities, the College-Level Examination Program offers 35 different subject tests falling under five separate general categories: Composition and Literature, Foreign Languages, History and Social Sciences, Science and Mathematics, and Business.

4. WHAT ARE THE SUBJECT EXAMINATIONS?

The 35 CLEP tests offered by the College Board are listed below:

COMPOSITION AND LITERATURE:
- American Literature
- Analyzing and Interpreting Literature
- English Composition
- English Composition with Essay
- English Literature
- Freshman College Composition
- Humanities

FOREIGN LANGUAGES
- French
- German
- Spanish

HISTORY AND SOCIAL SCIENCES
- American Government
- Introduction to Educational Psychology
- History of the United States I: Early Colonization to 1877
- History of the United States II: 1865 to the Present
- Human Growth and Development
- Principles of Macroeconomics
- Principles of Microeconomics
- Introductory Psychology
- Social Sciences and History
- Introductory Sociology
- Western Civilization I: Ancient Near East to 1648
- Western Civilization II: 1648 to the Present

SCIENCE AND MATHEMATICS
- College Algebra
- College Algebra-Trigonometry
- Biology
- Calculus
- Chemistry
- College Mathematics
- Natural Sciences
- Trigonometry
- Precalculus

BUSINESS
- Financial Accounting
- Introductory Business Law
- Information Systems and Computer Applications
- Principles of Management
- Principles of Marketing

CLEP Examinations cover material taught in courses that most students take as requirements in the first two years of college. A college usually grants the same amount of credit to students earning satisfactory scores on the CLEP examination as it grants to students successfully completing the equivalent course.

Many examinations are designed to correspond to one-semester courses; some, however, correspond to full-year or two-year courses.

Each exam is 90 minutes long and, except for English Composition with Essay, is made up primarily of multiple-choice questions. Some tests have several other types of questions besides multiple choice. To see a more detailed description of a particular CLEP exam, visit www.collegeboard.com/clep.

The English Composition with Essay exam is the only exam that includes a required essay. This essay is scored by college English faculty designated by CLEP and does not require an additional fee. However, other Composition and Literature tests offer optional essays, which some college and universities require and some do not. These essays are graded by faculty at the individual institutions that require them and require an additional $10 fee. Contact the particular institution to ask about essay requirements, and check with your test center for further details.

All 35 CLEP examinations are administered on computer. If you are unfamiliar with taking a test on a computer, consult the CLEP Sampler online at www.collegeboard.com/clep. The Sampler contains the same tutorials as the actual exams and helps familiarize you with navigation and how to answer different types of questions.

Points are not deducted for wrong or skipped answers – you receive one point for every correct answer. Therefore it is best that an answer is supplied for each exam question, whether it is a guess or not. The number of correct answers is then converted to a formula score. This formula, or "scaled," score is determined by a statistical process called *equating*, which adjusts for slight differences in difficulty between test forms and ensures that your score does not depend on the specific test form you took or how well others did on the same form. The scaled scores range from 20 to 80 – this is the number that will appear on your score report.

To ensure that you complete all questions in the time allotted, you would probably be wise to skip the more difficult or perplexing questions and return to them later. Although the multiple-choice items in these tests are carefully designed so as not to be tricky, misleading, or ambiguous, on the other hand, they are not all direct questions of factual information. They attempt, in their way, to elicit a response that indicates your knowledge or lack of knowledge of the material in question or your ability or inability to use or interpret a fact or idea. Thus, you should concentrate on answering the questions as they appear to be without attempting to out-guess the testmakers.

5. WHAT ARE THE FEES?

The fee for all CLEP examinations is $55. Optional essays required by some institutions are an additional $10.

6. WHEN ARE THE TESTS GIVEN?

CLEP tests are administered year-round. Consult the CLEP website (www.collegeboard.com/clep) and individual test centers for specific information.

7. WHERE ARE THE TESTS GIVEN?

More than 1,300 test centers are located on college and university campuses throughout the country, and additional centers are being established to meet increased needs. Any accredited collegiate institution with an explicit and publicly available policy of credit by examination can become a CLEP test center. To obtain a list of these centers, visit the CLEP website at www.collegeboard.com/clep.

8. HOW DO I REGISTER FOR THE COLLEGE-LEVEL EXAMINATION PROGRAM?

Contact an individual test center for information regarding registration, scheduling and fees. Registration/admission forms can also be obtained on the CLEP website.

9. MAY I REPEAT THE COLLEGE-LEVEL EXAMINATIONS?

You may repeat any examination providing at least six months have passed since you were last administered this test. If you repeat a test within a period of time less than six months, your scores will be cancelled and your fees forfeited. To repeat a test, check the appropriate space on the registration form.

10. WHEN MAY I EXPECT MY SCORE REPORTS?

With the exception of the English Composition with Essay exam, you should receive your score report instantly once the test is complete.

11. HOW SHOULD I PREPARE FOR THE COLLEGE-LEVEL EXAMINATIONS?

This book has been specifically designed to prepare candidates for these examinations. It will help you to consider, study, and review important content, principles, practices, procedures, problems, and techniques in the form of varied and concrete applications.

12. QUESTIONS AND ANSWERS APPEARING IN THIS PUBLICATION

The College-Level Examinations are offered by the College Board. Since copies of past examinations have not been made available, we have used equivalent materials, including questions and answers, which are highly recommended by us as an appropriate means of preparing for these examinations.

If you need additional information about CLEP Examinations, visit www.collegeboard.com/clep.

THE COLLEGE-LEVEL EXAMINATION PROGRAM

How The Program Works

CLEP examinations are administered at many colleges and universities across the country, and most institutions award college credit to those who do well on them. The examinations provide people who have acquired knowledge outside the usual educational settings the opportunity to show that they have learned college-level material without taking certain college courses.

The CLEP examinations cover material that is taught in introductory-level courses at many colleges and universities. Faculties at individual colleges review the tests to ensure that they cover the important material taught in their courses. Colleges differ in the examinations they accept; some colleges accept only two or three of the examinations while others accept nearly all of them.

Although CLEP is sponsored by the College Board and the examinations are scored by Educational Testing Service (ETS), neither of these organizations can award college credit. Only accredited colleges may grant credit toward a degree. When you take a CLEP examination, you may request that a copy of your score report be sent to the college you are attending or plan to attend. After evaluating your scores, the college will decide whether or not to award you credit for a certain course or courses, or to exempt you from them. If the college gives you credit, it will record the number of credits on your permanent record, thereby indicating that you have completed work equivalent to a course in that subject. If the college decides to grant exemption without giving you credit for a course, you will be permitted to omit a course that would normally be required of you and to take a course of your choice instead.

What the Examinations Are Like

The examinations consist mostly of multiple-choice questions to be answered within a 90-minute time limit. Additional information about each CLEP examination is given in the examination guide and on the CLEP website.

Where To Take the Examinations

CLEP examinations are administered throughout the year at the test centers of approximately 1,300 colleges and universities. On the CLEP website, you will find a list of institutions that award credit for satisfactory scores on CLEP examinations. Some colleges administer CLEP examinations to their own students only. Other institutions administer the tests to anyone who registers to take them. If your college does not administer the tests, contact the test centers in your area for information about its testing schedule.

Once you have been tested, your score report will be available instantly. CLEP scores are kept on file at ETS for 20 years; and during this period, for a small fee, you may have your transcript sent to another college or to anyone else you specify. (Your scores will never be sent to anyone without your approval.)

APPROACHING A COLLEGE ABOUT CLEP

The following sections provide a step-by-step approach to learning about the CLEP policy at a particular college or university. The person or office that can best assist students desiring CLEP credit may have a different title at each institution, but the following guidelines will lead you to information about CLEP at any institution.

Adults returning to college often benefit from special assistance when they approach a college. Opportunities for adults to return to formal learning in the classroom are now widespread, and colleges and universities have worked hard to make this a smooth process for older students. Many colleges have established special service offices that are staffed with trained professionals who understand the kinds of problems facing adults returning to college. If you think you might benefit from such assistance, be sure to find out whether these services are available at your college.

How to Apply for College Credit

STEP 1. Obtain the General Information Catalog and a copy of the CLEP policy from the colleges you are considering. If you have not yet applied for admission, ask for an admissions application form too.

Information about admissions and CLEP policies can be obtained by contacting college admissions offices or finding admissions information on the school websites. Tell the admissions officer that you are a prospective student and that you are interested in applying for admission and CLEP credit. Ask for a copy of the publication in which the college's complete CLEP policy is explained. Also get the name and the telephone number of the person to contact in case you have further questions about CLEP.

At this step, you may wish to obtain information from external degree colleges. Many adults find that such colleges suit their needs exceptionally well.

STEP 2. If you have not already been admitted to the college you are considering, look at its admission requirements for undergraduate students to see if you can qualify.

This is an important step because if you can't get into college, you can't get college credit for CLEP. Nearly all colleges require students to be admitted and to enroll in one or more courses before granting the students CLEP credit.

Virtually all public community colleges and a number of four-year state colleges have open admission policies for in-state students. This usually means that they admit anyone who has graduated from high school or has earned a high school equivalency diploma.

If you think you do not meet the admission requirements, contact the admissions office for an interview with a counselor. Colleges do sometimes make exceptions, particularly for adult applicants. State why you want the interview and ask what documents you should bring with you or send in advance. (These materials may include a high school transcript, transcript of previous college work, completed application for admission, etc.) Make an extra effort to have all the information requested in time for the interview.

During the interview, relax and be yourself. Be prepared to state honestly why you think you are ready and able to do college work. If you have already taken CLEP examinations and scored high enough to earn credit, you have shown that you are able to do college work. Mention this achievement to the admissions counselor because it may increase your chances of being accepted. If you have not taken a CLEP examination, you can still improve your chances of being accepted by describing how your job training or independent study has helped prepare you for college-level work. Tell the counselor what you have learned from your work and personal experiences.

STEP 3. Evaluate the college's CLEP policy.

Typically, a college lists all its academic policies, including CLEP policies, in its general catalog. You will probably find the CLEP policy statement under a heading such as Credit-by-Examination, Advanced Standing, Advanced Placement, or External Degree Program. These sections can usually be found in the front of the catalog.

Many colleges publish their credit-by-examination policies in a separate brochure, which is distributed through the campus testing office, counseling center, admissions office, or registrar's office. If you find a very general policy statement in the college catalog, seek clarification from one of these offices.

Review the material in the section of this guide entitled Questions to Ask About a College's CLEP Policy. Use these guidelines to evaluate the college's CLEP policy. If you have not yet taken a CLEP examination, this evaluation will help you decide which examinations to take and whether or not to take the free-response or essay portion. Because individual colleges have different CLEP policies, a review of several policies may help you decide which college to attend.

STEP 4. If you have not yet applied for admission, do so early.

Most colleges expect you to apply for admission several months before you enroll, and it is essential that you meet the published application deadlines. It takes time to process your application for admission; and if you have yet to take a CLEP examination, it will be some time before the college receives and reviews your score report. You will probably want to take some, if not all, of the CLEP examinations you are interested in before you enroll so you know which courses you need not register for. In fact, some colleges require that all CLEP scores be submitted before a student registers.

Complete all forms and include all documents requested with your application(s) for admission. Normally, an admissions decision cannot be reached until all documents have been submitted and evaluated. Unless told to do so, do not send your CLEP scores until you have been officially admitted.

STEP 5. Arrange to take CLEP examination(s) or to submit your CLEP score(s).

You may want to wait to take your CLEP examinations until you know definitely which college you will be attending. Then you can make sure you are taking tests your college will accept for credit. You will also be able to request that your scores be sent to the college, free of charge, when you take the tests.

If you have already taken CLEP examinations, but did not have a copy of your score report sent to your college, you may request the College Board to send an official transcript at any time for a small fee. Use the Transcript Request Form that was sent to you with your score report. If you do not have the form, you may find it online at www.collegeboard.com/clep.

Your CLEP scores will be evaluated, probably by someone in the admissions office, and sent to the registrar's office to be posted on your permanent record once you are enrolled. Procedures vary from college to college, but the process usually begins in the admissions office.

STEP 6. Ask to receive a written notice of the credit you receive for your CLEP score(s).

A written notice may save you problems later, when you submit your degree plan or file for graduation. In the event that there is a question about whether or not you earned CLEP credit, you will have an official record of what credit was awarded. You may also need this verification of course credit if you go for academic counseling before the credit is posted on your permanent record.

STEP 7. Before you register for courses, seek academic counseling.

A discussion with your academic advisor can prevent you from taking unnecessary courses and can tell you specifically what your CLEP credit will mean to you. This step may be accomplished at the time you enroll. Most colleges have orientation sessions for new students prior to each enrollment period. During orientation, students are usually assigned an academic advisor who then gives them individual help in developing long-range plans and a course schedule for the next semester. In conjunction with this counseling, you may be asked to take some additional tests so that you can be placed at the proper course level.

External Degree Programs

If you have acquired a considerable amount of college-level knowledge through job experience, reading, or noncredit courses, if you have accumulated college credits at a variety of colleges over a period of years, or if you prefer studying on your own rather than in a classroom setting, you may want to investigate the possibility of enrolling in an external degree program. Many colleges offer external degree programs that allow you to earn a degree by passing examinations (including CLEP), transferring credit from other colleges, and demonstrating in other ways that you have satisfied the educational requirements. No classroom attendance is required, and the programs are open to out-of-state candidates as well as residents. Thomas A. Edison State College in New Jersey and Charter Oaks College in Connecticut are fully accredited independent state colleges; the New York program is part of the state university system and is also fully accredited. If you are interested in exploring an external degree, you can write for more information to:

Charter Oak College
The Exchange, Suite 171
270 Farmington Avenue
Farmington, CT 06032-1909

Regents External Degree Program
Cultural Education Center
Empire State Plaza
Albany, New York 12230

Thomas A. Edison State College
101 West State Street
Trenton, New Jersey 08608

Many other colleges also have external degree or weekend programs. While they often require that a number of courses be taken on campus, the external degree programs tend to be more flexible in transferring credit, granting credit-by-examination, and allowing independent study than other traditional programs. When applying to a college, you may wish to ask whether it has an external degree or weekend program.

Questions to Ask About a College's CLEP Policy

Before taking CLEP examinations for the purpose of earning college credit, try to find the answers to these questions:

1. Which CLEP examinations are accepted by this college?

A college may accept some CLEP examinations for credit and not others - possibly not the one you are considering. The English faculty may decide to grant college English credit based on the CLEP English Composition examination, but not on the Freshman College Composition examination. Or, the mathematics faculty may decide to grant credit based on the College Mathematics to non-mathematics majors only, requiring majors to take an examination in algebra, trigonometry, or calculus to earn credit. For these reasons, it is important that you know the specific CLEP tests for which you can receive credit.

2. Does the college require the optional free-response (essay) section as well as the objective portion of the CLEP examination you are considering?

Knowing the answer to this question ahead of time will permit you to schedule the optional essay examination when you register to take your CLEP examination.

3. Is credit granted for specific courses? If so, which ones?

You are likely to find that credit will be granted for specific courses and the course titles will be designated in the college's CLEP policy. It is not necessary, however, that credit be granted for a specific course in order for you to benefit from your CLEP credit. For instance, at many liberal arts colleges, all students must take certain types of courses; these courses may be labeled the core curriculum, general education requirements, distribution requirements, or liberal arts requirements. The requirements are often expressed in terms of credit hours. For example, all students may be required to take at least six hours of humanities, six hours of English, three hours of mathematics, six hours of natural science, and six hours of social science, with no particular courses in these disciplines specified. In these instances, CLEP credit may be given as 6 hrs. English credit or 3 hrs. Math credit without specifying for which English or mathematics courses credit has been awarded. In order to avoid possible disappointment, you should know before taking a CLEP examination what type of credit you can receive and whether you will only be exempted from a required course but receive no credit.

4. How much credit is granted for each examination you are considering, and does the college place a limit on the total amount of CLEP credit you can earn toward your degree?

Not all colleges that grant CLEP credit award the same amount for individual tests. Furthermore, some colleges place a limit on the total amount of credit you can earn through CLEP or other examinations. Other colleges may grant you exemption but no credit toward your degree. Knowing several colleges' policies concerning these issues may help you decide which college you will attend. If you think you are capable of passing a number of CLEP examinations, you may want to attend a college that will allow you to earn credit for all or most of them. For example, the state external degree programs grant credit for most CLEP examinations (and other tests as well).

5. What is the required score for earning CLEP credit for each test you are considering?

Most colleges publish the required scores or percentile ranks for earning CLEP credit in their general catalog or in a brochure. The required score may vary from test to test, so find out the required score for each test you are considering.

6. What is the college's policy regarding prior course work in the subject in which you are considering taking a CLEP test?

Some colleges will not grant credit for a CLEP test if the student has already attempted a college-level course closely aligned with that test. For example, if you successfully completed English 101 or a comparable course on another campus, you will probably not be permitted to receive CLEP credit in that subject, too. Some colleges will not permit you to earn CLEP credit for a course that you failed.

7. Does the college make additional stipulations before credit will be granted?

It is common practice for colleges to award CLEP credit only to their enrolled students. There are other stipulations, however, that vary from college to college. For example, does the college require you to formally apply for or accept CLEP credit by completing and signing a form? Or does the college require you to validate your CLEP score by successfully completing a more advanced course in the subject? Answers to these and other questions will help to smooth the process of earning college credit through CLEP.

The above questions and the discussions that follow them indicate some of the ways in which colleges' CLEP policies can vary. Find out as much as possible about the CLEP policies at the colleges you are interested in so you can choose a college with a policy that is compatible with your educational goals. Once you have selected the college you will attend, you can find out which CLEP examinations your college recognizes and the requirements for earning CLEP credit.

DECIDING WHICH EXAMINATIONS TO TAKE

If You're Taking the Examinations for College Credit or Career Advancement:

Most people who take CLEP examinations do so in order to earn credit for college courses. Others take the examinations in order to qualify for job promotions or for professional certification or licensing. It is vital to most candidates who are taking the tests for any of these reasons that they be well prepared for the tests they are taking so that they can advance as rapidly as possible toward their educational or career goals.

It is usually advisable that those who have limited knowledge in the subjects covered by the tests they are considering enroll in the college courses in which that material is taught. Those who are uncertain about whether or not they know enough about a subject to do well on a particular CLEP test will find the following guidelines helpful.

There is no way to predict if you will pass a particular CLEP examination, but answers to the questions under the seven headings below should give you an indication of whether or not you are likely to succeed.

1. Test Descriptions

Read the description of the test provided. Are you familiar with most of the topics and terminology in the outline?

2. Textbooks

Examine the suggested textbooks and other resource materials following the test descriptions in this guide. Have you recently read one or more of these books, or have you read similar college-level books on this subject? If you have not, read through one or more of the textbooks listed, or through the textbook used for this course at your college. Are you familiar with most of the topics and terminology in the book?

3. Sample Questions

The sample questions provided are intended to be typical of the content and difficulty of the questions on the test. Although they are not an exact miniature of the test, the proportion of the sample questions you can answer correctly should be a rough estimate of the proportion of questions you will be able to answer correctly on the test.

Answer as many of the sample questions for this test as you can. Check your answers against the correct answers. Did you answer more than half the questions correctly?

Because of variations in course content at different institutions, and because questions on CLEP tests vary from easy to difficult - with most being of moderate difficulty - the average student who passes a course in a subject can usually answer correctly about half the questions on the corresponding CLEP examination. Most colleges set their passing scores near this level, but some set them higher. If your college has set its required score above the level required by most colleges, you may need to answer a larger proportion of questions on the test correctly.

4. Previous Study

Have you taken noncredit courses in this subject offered by an adult school or a private school, through correspondence, or in connection with your job? Did you do exceptionally well in this subject in high school, or did you take an honors course in this subject?

5. Experience

Have you learned or used the knowledge or skills included in this test in your job or life experience? For example, if you lived in a Spanish-speaking country and spoke the language for a year or more, you might consider taking the Spanish examination. Or, if you have worked at a job in which you used accounting and finance skills, Principles of Accounting would be a likely test for you to take. Or, if you have read a considerable amount of literature and attended many art exhibits, concerts, and plays, you might expect to do well on the Humanities exam.

6. Other Examinations

Have you done well on other standardized tests in subjects related to the one you want to take? For example, did you score well above average on a portion of a college entrance examination covering similar skills, or did you obtain an exceptionally high score on a high school equivalency test or a licensing examination in this subject? Although such tests do not cover exactly the same material as the CLEP examinations and may be easier, persons who do well on these tests often do well on CLEP examinations, too.

7. Advice

Has a college counselor, professor, or some other professional person familiar with your ability advised you to take a CLEP examination?

If your answer was yes to questions under several of the above headings, you probably have a good chance of passing the CLEP examination you are considering. It is unlikely that you would have acquired sufficient background from experience alone. Learning gained through reading and study is essential, and you will probably find some additional study helpful before taking a CLEP examination.

If You're Taking the Examinations to Prepare for College

Many people entering college, particularly adults returning to college after several years away from formal education, are uncertain about their ability to compete with other college students. They wonder whether they have sufficient background for college study, and those who have been away from formal study for some time wonder whether they have forgotten how to study, how to take tests, and how to write papers. Such people may wish to improve their test-taking and study skills prior to enrolling in courses.

One way to assess your ability to perform at the college level and to improve your test-taking and study skills at the same time is to prepare for and take one or more CLEP examinations. You need not be enrolled in a college to take a CLEP examination, and you may have your scores sent only to yourself and later request that a transcript be sent to a college if you then decide to apply for credit. By reviewing the test descriptions and sample questions, you may find one or several subject areas in which you think you have substantial knowledge. Select one examination, or more if you like, and carefully read at least one of the textbooks listed in the bibliography for the test. By doing this, you will get a better idea of how much you know of what is usually taught in a college-level course in that subject. Study as much material as you can, until you think you have a good grasp of the subject matter. Then take the test at a college in your area. It will be several weeks before you receive your results, and you may wish to begin reviewing for another test in the meantime.

To find out if you are eligible for credit for your CLEP score, you must compare your score with the score required by the college you plan to attend. If you are not yet sure which college you will attend, or whether you will enroll in college at all, you should begin to follow the steps outlined. It is best that you do this before taking a CLEP test, but if you are taking the test only for the experience and to familiarize yourself with college-level material and requirements, you might take the test before you approach a college. Even if the college you decide to attend does not accept the test you took, the experience of taking such a test will enable you to meet with greater confidence the requirements of courses you will take.

You will find information about how to interpret your scores in WHAT YOUR SCORES MEAN, which you will receive with your score report, and which can also be found online at the CLEP website. Many colleges follow the recommendations of the American Council on Education (ACE) for setting their required scores, so you can use this information as a guide in determining how well you did. The ACE recommendations are included in the booklet.

If you do not do well enough on the test to earn college credit, don't be discouraged. Usually, it is the best college students who are exempted from courses or receive credit-by-examination. The fact that you cannot get credit for your score means that you should probably enroll in a college course to learn the material. However, if your score was close to the required score, or if you feel you could do better on a second try or after some additional study, you may retake the test after six months. Do not take it sooner or your score will not be reported and your fee will be forfeited.

If you do earn the score required to earn credit, you will have demonstrated that you already have some college-level knowledge. You will also have a better idea whether you should take additional CLEP examinations. And, what is most important, you can enroll in college with confidence, knowing that you do have the ability to succeed.

PREPARING TO TAKE CLEP EXAMINATIONS

Having made the decision to take one or more CLEP examinations, most people then want to know if it is worthwhile to prepare for them - how much, how long, when, and how should they go about it? The precise answers to these questions vary greatly from individual to individual. However, most candidates find that some type of test preparation is helpful.

Most people who take CLEP examinations do so to show that they have already learned the important material that is taught in a college course. Many of them need only a quick review to assure themselves that they have not forgotten some of what they once studied, and to fill in some of the gaps in their knowledge of the subject. Others feel that they need a thorough review and spend several weeks studying for a test. A few wish to take a CLEP examination as a kind of final examination for independent study of a subject instead of the college course. This last group requires significantly more study than those who only need to review, and they may need some guidance from professors of the subjects they are studying.

The key to how you prepare for CLEP examinations often lies in locating those skills and areas of prior learning in which you are strong and deciding where to focus your energies. Some people may know a great deal about a certain subject area, but may not test well. These individuals would probably be just as concerned about strengthening their test-taking skills as they are about studying for a specific test. Many mental and physical skills are used in preparing for a test. It is important not only to review or study for the examinations, but to make certain that you are alert, relatively free of anxiety, and aware of how to approach standardized tests. Suggestions on developing test-taking skills and preparing psychologically and physically for a test are given. The following section suggests ways of assessing your knowledge of the content of a test and then reviewing and studying the material.

Using This Study Guide

Begin by carefully reading the test description and outline of knowledge and skills required for the examination, if given. As you read through the topics listed there, ask yourself how much you know about each one. Also note the terms, names, and symbols that are mentioned, and ask yourself whether you are familiar with them. This will give you a quick overview of how much you know about the subject. If you are familiar with nearly all the material, you will probably need a minimum of review; however, if less than half of it is familiar, you will probably require substantial study to do well on the test.

If, after reviewing the test description, you find that you need extensive review, delay answering the sample question until you have done some reading in the subject. If you complete them before reviewing the material, you will probably look for the answers as you study, and then they will not be a good assessment of your ability at a later date.

If you think you are familiar with most of the test material, try to answer the sample questions.

Apply the test-taking strategies given. Keeping within the time limit suggested will give you a rough idea of how quickly you should work in order to complete the actual test.

Check your answers against the answer key. If you answered nearly all the questions correctly, you probably do not need to study the subject extensively. If you got about half the questions correct, you ought o review at least one textbook or other suggested materials on the subject. If you answered less than half the questions correctly, you will probably benefit from more extensive reading in the subject and thorough study of one or more textbooks. The textbooks listed are used at many colleges but they are not the only good texts. You will find helpful almost any standard text available to you., such as the textbook used at your college, or earlier editions of texts listed. For some examinations, topic outlines and textbooks may not be available. Take the sample tests in this book and check your answers at the end of each test. Check wrong answers.

Suggestions for Studying

The following suggestions have been gathered from people who have prepared for CLEP examinations or other college-level tests.

1. Define your goals and locate study materials

First, determine your study goals. Set aside a block of time to review the material provided in this book, and then decide which test(s) you will take. Using the suggestions, locate suitable resource materials. If a preparation course is offered by an adult school or college in your area, you might find it helpful to enroll.

2. Find a good place to study

To determine what kind of place you need for studying, ask yourself questions such as: Do I need a quiet place? Does the telephone distract me? Do objects I see in this place remind me of things I should do? Is it too warm? Is it well lit? Am I too comfortable here? Do I have space to spread out my materials? You may find the library more conducive to studying than your home. If you decide to study at home, you might prevent interruptions by other household members by putting a sign on the door of your study room to indicate when you will be available.

3. Schedule time to study

To help you determine where studying best fits into your schedule, try this exercise: Make a list of your daily activities (for example, sleeping, working, and eating) and estimate how many hours per day you spend on each activity. Now, rate all the activities on your list in order of their importance and evaluate your use of time. Often people are astonished at how an average day appears from this perspective. They may discover that they were unaware how large portions of time are spent, or they learn their time can be scheduled in alternative ways. For example, they can remove the least important activities from their day and devote that time to studying or another important activity.

4. Establish a study routine and a set of goals

In order to study effectively, you should establish specific goals and a schedule for accomplishing them. Some people find it helpful to write out a weekly schedule and cross out each study period when it is completed. Others maintain their concentration better by writing down the time when they expect to complete a study task. Most people find short periods of intense study more productive than long stretches of time. For example, they may follow a regular schedule of several 20- or 30-minute study periods with short breaks between them. Some people like to allow themselves rewards as they complete each study goal. It is not essential that you accomplish every goal exactly within your schedule; the point is to be committed to your task.

5. Learn how to take an active role in studying.

If you have not done much studying for some time, you may find it difficult to concentrate at first. Try a method of studying, such as the one outlined below, that will help you concentrate on and remember what you read.

    a. First, read the chapter summary and the introduction. Then you will know what to look for in your reading.

    b. Next, convert the section or paragraph headlines into questions. For example, if you are reading a section entitled, The Causes of the American Revolution, ask yourself: *What were the causes of the American Revolution?* Compose the answer as you read the paragraph. Reading and answering questions aloud will help you understand and remember the material.

c. Take notes on key ideas or concepts as you read. Writing will also help you fix concepts more firmly in your mind. Underlining key ideas or writing notes in your book can be helpful and will be useful for review. Underline only important points. If you underline more than a third of each paragraph, you are probably underlining too much.

d. If there are questions or problems at the end of a chapter, answer or solve them on paper as if you were asked to do them for homework. Mathematics textbooks (and some other books) sometimes include answers to some or all of the exercises. If you have such a book, write your answers before looking at the ones given. When problem-solving is involved, work enough problems to master the required methods and concepts. If you have difficulty with problems, review any sample problems or explanations in the chapter.

e. To retain knowledge, most people have to review the material periodically. If you are preparing for a test over an extended period of time, review key concepts and notes each week or so. Do not wait for weeks to review the material or you will need to relearn much of it.

Psychological and Physical Preparation

Most people feel at least some nervousness before taking a test. Adults who are returning to college may not have taken a test in many years or they may have had little experience with standardized tests. Some younger students, as well, are uncomfortable with testing situations. People who received their education in countries outside the United States may find that many tests given in this country are quite different from the ones they are accustomed to taking.

Not only might candidates find the types of tests and the kinds of questions on them unfamiliar, but other aspects of the testing environment may be strange as well. The physical and mental stress that results from meeting this new experience can hinder a candidate's ability to demonstrate his or her true degree of knowledge in the subject area being tested. For this reason, it is important to go to the test center well prepared, both mentally and physically, for taking the test. You may find the following suggestions helpful.

1. Familiarize yourself, as much as possible, with the test and the test situation before the day of the examination. It will be helpful for you to know ahead of time:

    a. How much time will be allowed for the test and whether there are timed subsections.

    b. What types of questions and directions appear on the examination.

    c. How your test score will be computed.

    d. How to properly answer the questions on the computer (See the CLEP Sample on the CLEP website)

e. In which building and room the examination will be administered. If you don't know where the building is, locate it or get directions ahead of time.

f. The time of the test administration. You might wish to confirm this information a day or two before the examination and find out what time the building and room will be open so that you can plan to arrive early.

g. Where to park your car or, if you wish to take public transportation, which bus or train to take and the location of the nearest stop.

h. Whether smoking will be permitted during the test.

i. Whether there will be a break between examinations (if you will be taking more than one on the same day), and whether there is a place nearby where you can get something to eat or drink.

2. Go to the test situation relaxed and alert. In order to prepare for the test:

a. Get a good night's sleep. Last minute cramming, particularly late the night before, is usually counterproductive.

b. Eat normally. It is usually not wise to skip breakfast or lunch on the day of the test or to eat a big meal just before the test.

c. Avoid tranquilizers and stimulants. If you follow the other directions in this book, you won't need artificial aids. It's better to be a little tense than to be drowsy, but stimulants such as coffee and cola can make you nervous and interfere with your concentration.

d. Don't drink a lot of liquids before the test. Having to leave the room during the test will disturb your concentration and take valuable time away from the test.

e. If you are inclined to be nervous or tense, learn some relaxation exercises and use them before and perhaps during the test.

3. Arrive for the test early and prepared. Be sure to:

a. Arrive early enough so that you can find a parking place, locate the test center, and get settled comfortably before testing begins. Allow some extra time in case you are delayed unexpectedly.

b. Take the following with you:

- Your completed Registration/Admission Form
- Two forms of identification – one being a government-issued photo ID with signature, such as a driver's license or passport
- Non-mechanical pencil
- A watch so that you can time your progress (digital watches are prohibited)
- Your glasses if you need them for reading or seeing the chalkboard or wall clock

c. Leave all books, papers, and notes outside the test center. You will not be permitted to use your own scratch paper; it will be provided. Also prohibited are calculators, cell phones, beepers, pagers, photo/copy devices, radios, headphones, food, beverages, and several other items.

d. Be prepared for any temperature in the testing room. Wear layers of clothing that can be removed if the room is too hot but will keep you warm if it is too cold.

4. When you enter the test room:

a. Sit in a seat that provides a maximum of comfort and freedom from distraction.

b. Read directions carefully, and listen to all instructions given by the test administrator. If you don't understand the directions, ask for help before test timing begins. If you must ask a question after the test has begun, raise your hand and a proctor will assist you. The proctor can answer certain kinds of questions but cannot help you with the test.

c. Know your rights as a test taker. You can expect to be given the full working time allowed for the test(s) and a reasonably quiet and comfortable place in which to work. If a poor test situation is preventing you from doing your best, ask if the situation can be remedied. If bad test conditions cannot be remedied, ask the person in charge to report the problem in the Irregularity Report that will be sent to ETS with the answer sheets. You may also wish to contact CLEP. Describe the exact circumstances as completely as you can. Be sure to include the test date and name(s) of the test(s) you took. ETS will investigate the problem to make sure it does not happen again, and, if the problem is serious enough, may arrange for you to retake the test without charge.

TAKING THE EXAMINATIONS

A person may know a great deal about the subject being tested, but not do as well as he or she is capable of on the test. Knowing how to approach a test is an important part of the testing process. While a command of test-taking skills cannot substitute for knowledge of the subject matter, it can be a significant factor in successful testing.

Test-taking skills enable a person to use all available information to earn a score that truly reflects his or her ability. There are different strategies for approaching different kinds of test questions. For example, free-response questions require a very different tack than do multiple-choice questions. Other factors, such as how the test will be graded, may also influence your approach to the test and your use of test time. Thus, your preparation for a test should include finding out all you can about the test so that you can use the most effective test-taking strategies.

Before taking a test, you should know approximately how many questions are on the test, how much time you will be allowed, how the test will be scored or graded, what types of questions and directions are on the test, and how you will be required to record your answers.

Taking Multiple-Choice Tests

1. Listen carefully to the instructions given by the test administrator and read carefully all directions before you begin to answer the questions.

2. Note the time that the test administrator starts timing the test. As you proceed, make sure that you are not working too slowly. You should have answered at least half the questions in a section when half the time for that section has passed. If you have not reached that point in the section, speed up your pace on the remaining questions.

3. Before answering a question, read the entire question, including all the answer choices. Don't think that because the first or second answer choice looks good to you, it isn't necessary to read the remaining options. Instructions usually tell you to select the best answer. Sometimes one answer choice is partially correct, but another option is better; therefore, it is usually a good idea to read all the answers before you choose one.

4. Read and consider every question. Questions that look complicated at first glance may not actually be so difficult once you have read them carefully.

5. Do not puzzle too long over any one question. If you don't know the answer after you've considered it briefly, go on to the next question. Make sure you return to the question later.

6. Make sure you record your response properly.

7. In trying to determine the correct answer, you may find it helpful to cross out those options that you know are incorrect, and to make marks next to those you think might be correct. If you decide to skip the question and come back to it later, you will save yourself the time of reconsidering all the options.

8. Watch for the following key words in test questions:

all	generally	never	perhaps
always	however	none	rarely
but	may	not	seldom
except	must	often	sometimes
every	necessary	only	usually

When a question or answer option contains words such as always, every, only, never, and none, there can be no exceptions to the answer you choose. Use of words such as often, rarely, sometimes, and generally indicates that there may be some exceptions to the answer.

9. Do not waste your time looking for clues to right answers based on flaws in question wording or patterns in correct answers. Professionals at the College Board and ETS put

a great deal of effort into developing valid, reliable, fair tests. CLEP test development committees are composed of college faculty who are experts in the subject covered by the test and are appointed by the College Board to write test questions and to scrutinize each question that is included on a CLEP test. Committee members make every effort to ensure that the questions are not ambiguous, that they have only one correct answer, and that they cover college-level topics. These committees do not intentionally include trick questions. If you think a question is flawed, ask the test administrator to report it, or contact CLEP immediately.

Taking Free-Response or Essay Tests

If your college requires the optional free-response or essay portion of a CLEP Composition and Literature exams, you should do some additional preparation for your CLEP test. Taking an essay test is very different from taking a multiple-choice test, so you will need to use some other strategies.

The essay written as part of the English Composition and Essay exam is graded by English professors from a variety of colleges and universities. A process called holistic scoring is used to rate your writing ability.

The optional free-response essays, on the other hand, are graded by the faculty of the college you designate as a score recipient. Guidelines and criteria for grading essays are not specified by the College Board or ETS. You may find it helpful, therefore, to talk with someone at your college to find out what criteria will be used to determine whether you will get credit. If the test requires essay responses, ask how much emphasis will be placed on your writing ability and your ability to organize your thoughts as opposed to your knowledge of subject matter. Find out how much weight will be given to your multiple-choice test score in comparison with your free-response grade in determining whether you will get credit. This will give you an idea where you should expend the greatest effort in preparing for and taking the test.

Here are some strategies you will find useful in taking any essay test:

1. Before you begin to write, read all questions carefully and take a few minutes to jot down some ideas you might include in each answer.

2. If you are given a choice of questions to answer, choose the questions you think you can answer most clearly and knowledgeably.

3. Determine in what order you will answer the questions. Answer those you find the easiest first so that any extra time can be spent on the more difficult questions.

4. When you know which questions you will answer and in what order, determine how much testing time remains and estimate how many minutes you will devote to each question. Unless suggested times are given for the questions or one question appears to require more or less time than the others, allot an equal amount of time to each question.

5. Before answering each question, indicate the number of the question as it is given in the test book. You need not copy the entire question from the question sheet, but it will be helpful to you and to the person grading your test if you indicate briefly the topic you are addressing – particularly if you are not answering the questions in the order in which they appear on the test.

6. Before answering each question, read it again carefully to make sure you are interpreting it correctly. Underline key words, such as those listed below, that often appear in free-response questions. Be sure you know the exact meaning of these words before taking the test.

analyze	demonstrate	enumerate	list
apply	derive	explain	outline
assess	describe	generalize	prove
compare	determine	illustrate	rank
contrast	discuss	interpret	show
define	distinguish	justify	summarize

If a question asks you to outline, define, or summarize, do not write a detailed explanation; if a question asks you to analyze, explain, illustrate, interpret, or show, you must do more than briefly describe the topic.

For a current listing of CLEP Colleges

where you can get credit and be tested, write:

CLEP, P.O. Box 6600, Princeton, NJ 08541-6600

Or e-mail: clep@ets.org, or call: (609) 771-7865

HOW TO TAKE A TEST

You have studied long, hard and conscientiously.

With your official admission card in hand, and your heart pounding, you have been admitted to the examination room.

You note that there are several hundred other applicants in the examination room waiting to take the same test.

They all appear to be equally well prepared.

You know that nothing but your best effort will suffice. The "moment of truth" is at hand: you now have to demonstrate objectively, in writing, your knowledge of content and your understanding of subject matter.

You are fighting the most important battle of your life—to pass and/or score high on an examination which will determine your career and provide the economic basis for your livelihood.

What extra, special things should you know and should you do in taking the examination?

I. YOU MUST PASS AN EXAMINATION

A. WHAT EVERY CANDIDATE SHOULD KNOW
Examination applicants often ask us for help in preparing for the written test. What can I study in advance? What kinds of questions will be asked? How will the test be given? How will the papers be graded?

B. HOW ARE EXAMS DEVELOPED?
Examinations are carefully written by trained technicians who are specialists in the field known as "psychological measurement," in consultation with recognized authorities in the field of work that the test will cover. These experts recommend the subject matter areas or skills to be tested; only those knowledges or skills important to your success on the job are included. The most reliable books and source materials available are used as references. Together, the experts and technicians judge the difficulty level of the questions.
Test technicians know how to phrase questions so that the problem is clearly stated. Their ethics do not permit "trick" or "catch" questions. Questions may have been tried out on sample groups, or subjected to statistical analysis, to determine their usefulness.
Written tests are often used in combination with performance tests, ratings of training and experience, and oral interviews. All of these measures combine to form the best-known means of finding the right person for the right job.

II. HOW TO PASS THE WRITTEN TEST

A. BASIC STEPS

1) Study the announcement

How, then, can you know what subjects to study? Our best answer is: "Learn as much as possible about the class of positions for which you've applied." The exam will test the knowledge, skills and abilities needed to do the work.

Your most valuable source of information about the position you want is the official exam announcement. This announcement lists the training and experience qualifications. Check these standards and apply only if you come reasonably close to meeting them. Many jurisdictions preview the written test in the exam announcement by including a section called "Knowledge and Abilities Required," "Scope of the Examination," or some similar heading. Here you will find out specifically what fields will be tested.

2) Choose appropriate study materials

If the position for which you are applying is technical or advanced, you will read more advanced, specialized material. If you are already familiar with the basic principles of your field, elementary textbooks would waste your time. Concentrate on advanced textbooks and technical periodicals. Think through the concepts and review difficult problems in your field.

These are all general sources. You can get more ideas on your own initiative, following these leads. For example, training manuals and publications of the government agency which employs workers in your field can be useful, particularly for technical and professional positions. A letter or visit to the government department involved may result in more specific study suggestions, and certainly will provide you with a more definite idea of the exact nature of the position you are seeking.

3) Study this book!

III. KINDS OF TESTS

Tests are used for purposes other than measuring knowledge and ability to perform specified duties. For some positions, it is equally important to test ability to make adjustments to new situations or to profit from training. In others, basic mental abilities not dependent on information are essential. Questions which test these things may not appear as pertinent to the duties of the position as those which test for knowledge and information. Yet they are often highly important parts of a fair examination. For very general questions, it is almost impossible to help you direct your study efforts. What we can do is to point out some of the more common of these general abilities needed in public service positions and describe some typical questions.

1) General information

Broad, general information has been found useful for predicting job success in some kinds of work. This is tested in a variety of ways, from vocabulary lists to questions about current events. Basic background in some field of work, such as sociology or economics, may be sampled in a group of questions. Often these are principles which have become familiar to most persons through exposure rather than through formal training. It is difficult to advise you how to study for these questions; being alert to the world around you is our best suggestion.

2) Verbal ability

An example of an ability needed in many positions is verbal or language ability. Verbal ability is, in brief, the ability to use and understand words. Vocabulary and grammar tests are typical measures of this ability. Reading comprehension or paragraph interpretation questions are common in many kinds of civil service tests. You are given a paragraph of written material and asked to find its central meaning.

IV. KINDS OF QUESTIONS

1. Multiple-choice Questions

Most popular of the short-answer questions is the "multiple choice" or "best answer" question. It can be used, for example, to test for factual knowledge, ability to solve problems or judgment in meeting situations found at work.

A multiple-choice question is normally one of three types:
- It can begin with an incomplete statement followed by several possible endings. You are to find the one ending which best completes the statement, although some of the others may not be entirely wrong.
- It can also be a complete statement in the form of a question which is answered by choosing one of the statements listed.
- It can be in the form of a problem – again you select the best answer.

Here is an example of a multiple-choice question with a discussion which should give you some clues as to the method for choosing the right answer:

When an employee has a complaint about his assignment, the action which will best help him overcome his difficulty is to
    A. discuss his difficulty with his coworkers
    B. take the problem to the head of the organization
    C. take the problem to the person who gave him the assignment
    D. say nothing to anyone about his complaint

In answering this question, you should study each of the choices to find which is best. Consider choice "A" – Certainly an employee may discuss his complaint with fellow employees, but no change or improvement can result, and the complaint remains unresolved. Choice "B" is a poor choice since the head of the organization probably does not know what assignment you have been given, and taking your problem to him is known as "going over the head" of the supervisor. The supervisor, or person who made the assignment, is the person who can clarify it or correct any injustice. Choice "C" is, therefore, correct. To say nothing, as in choice "D," is unwise. Supervisors have and interest in knowing the problems employees are facing, and the employee is seeking a solution to his problem.

2. True/False

3. Matching Questions

Matching an answer from a column of choices within another column.

V. RECORDING YOUR ANSWERS

Computer terminals are used more and more today for many different kinds of exams.

For an examination with very few applicants, you may be told to record your answers in the test booklet itself. Separate answer sheets are much more common. If this separate answer sheet is to be scored by machine – and this is often the case – it is highly important that you mark your answers correctly in order to get credit.

VI. BEFORE THE TEST

YOUR PHYSICAL CONDITION IS IMPORTANT

If you are not well, you can't do your best work on tests. If you are half asleep, you can't do your best either. Here are some tips:

1) Get about the same amount of sleep you usually get. Don't stay up all night before the test, either partying or worrying—DON'T DO IT!
2) If you wear glasses, be sure to wear them when you go to take the test. This goes for hearing aids, too.
3) If you have any physical problems that may keep you from doing your best, be sure to tell the person giving the test. If you are sick or in poor health, you relay cannot do your best on any test. You can always come back and take the test some other time.

Common sense will help you find procedures to follow to get ready for an examination. Too many of us, however, overlook these sensible measures. Indeed, nervousness and fatigue have been found to be the most serious reasons why applicants fail to do their best on civil service tests. Here is a list of reminders:

- Begin your preparation early – Don't wait until the last minute to go scurrying around for books and materials or to find out what the position is all about.
- Prepare continuously – An hour a night for a week is better than an all-night cram session. This has been definitely established. What is more, a night a week for a month will return better dividends than crowding your study into a shorter period of time.
- Locate the place of the exam – You have been sent a notice telling you when and where to report for the examination. If the location is in a different town or otherwise unfamiliar to you, it would be well to inquire the best route and learn something about the building.
- Relax the night before the test – Allow your mind to rest. Do not study at all that night. Plan some mild recreation or diversion; then go to bed early and get a good night's sleep.
- Get up early enough to make a leisurely trip to the place for the test – This way unforeseen events, traffic snarls, unfamiliar buildings, etc. will not upset you.
- Dress comfortably – A written test is not a fashion show. You will be known by number and not by name, so wear something comfortable.
- Leave excess paraphernalia at home – Shopping bags and odd bundles will get in your way. You need bring only the items mentioned in the official notice you received; usually everything you need is provided. Do not bring reference books to the exam. They will only confuse those last minutes and be taken away from you when in the test room.

- Arrive somewhat ahead of time – If because of transportation schedules you must get there very early, bring a newspaper or magazine to take your mind off yourself while waiting.
- Locate the examination room – When you have found the proper room, you will be directed to the seat or part of the room where you will sit. Sometimes you are given a sheet of instructions to read while you are waiting. Do not fill out any forms until you are told to do so; just read them and be prepared.
- Relax and prepare to listen to the instructions
- If you have any physical problem that may keep you from doing your best, be sure to tell the test administrator. If you are sick or in poor health, you really cannot do your best on the exam. You can come back and take the test some other time.

VII. AT THE TEST

The day of the test is here and you have the test booklet in your hand. The temptation to get going is very strong. Caution! There is more to success than knowing the right answers. You must know how to identify your papers and understand variations in the type of short-answer question used in this particular examination. Follow these suggestions for maximum results from your efforts:

1) Cooperate with the monitor

The test administrator has a duty to create a situation in which you can be as much at ease as possible. He will give instructions, tell you when to begin, check to see that you are marking your answer sheet correctly, and so on. He is not there to guard you, although he will see that your competitors do not take unfair advantage. He wants to help you do your best.

2) Listen to all instructions

Don't jump the gun! Wait until you understand all directions. In most civil service tests you get more time than you need to answer the questions. So don't be in a hurry. Read each word of instructions until you clearly understand the meaning. Study the examples, listen to all announcements and follow directions. Ask questions if you do not understand what to do.

3) Identify your papers

Civil service exams are usually identified by number only. You will be assigned a number; you must not put your name on your test papers. Be sure to copy your number correctly. Since more than one exam may be given, copy your exact examination title.

4) Plan your time

Unless you are told that a test is a "speed" or "rate of work" test, speed itself is usually not important. Time enough to answer all the questions will be provided, but this does not mean that you have all day. An overall time limit has been set. Divide the total time (in minutes) by the number of questions to determine the approximate time you have for each question.

5) Do not linger over difficult questions

If you come across a difficult question, mark it with a paper clip (useful to have along) and come back to it when you have been through the booklet. One caution if you do this – be sure to skip a number on your answer sheet as well. Check often to be sure that you have not lost your place and that you are marking in the row numbered the same as the question you are answering.

6) Read the questions
   Be sure you know what the question asks! Many capable people are unsuccessful because they failed to read the questions correctly.

7) Answer all questions
   Unless you have been instructed that a penalty will be deducted for incorrect answers, it is better to guess than to omit a question.

8) Speed tests
   It is often better NOT to guess on speed tests. It has been found that on timed tests people are tempted to spend the last few seconds before time is called in marking answers at random – without even reading them – in the hope of picking up a few extra points. To discourage this practice, the instructions may warn you that your score will be "corrected" for guessing. That is, a penalty will be applied. The incorrect answers will be deducted from the correct ones, or some other penalty formula will be used.

9) Review your answers
   If you finish before time is called, go back to the questions you guessed or omitted to give them further thought. Review other answers if you have time.

10) Return your test materials
    If you are ready to leave before others have finished or time is called, take ALL your materials to the monitor and leave quietly. Never take any test material with you. The monitor can discover whose papers are not complete, and taking a test booklet may be grounds for disqualification.

VIII. EXAMINATION TECHNIQUES

1) Read the general instructions carefully. These are usually printed on the first page of the exam booklet. As a rule, these instructions refer to the timing of the examination; the fact that you should not start work until the signal and must stop work at a signal, etc. If there are any special instructions, such as a choice of questions to be answered, make sure that you note this instruction carefully.

2) When you are ready to start work on the examination, that is as soon as the signal has been given, read the instructions to each question booklet, underline any key words or phrases, such as least, best, outline, describe and the like. In this way you will tend to answer as requested rather than discover on reviewing your paper that you listed without describing, that you selected the worst choice rather than the best choice, etc.

3) If the examination is of the objective or multiple-choice type – that is, each question will also give a series of possible answers: A, B, C or D, and you are called upon to select the best answer and write the letter next to that answer on your answer paper – it is advisable to start answering each question in turn. There may be anywhere from 50 to 100 such questions in the three or four hours allotted and you can see how much time would be taken if you read through all the questions before beginning to answer any. Furthermore, if you

come across a question or group of questions which you know would be difficult to answer, it would undoubtedly affect your handling of all the other questions.

4) If the examination is of the essay type and contains but a few questions, it is a moot point as to whether you should read all the questions before starting to answer any one. Of course, if you are given a choice – say five out of seven and the like – then it is essential to read all the questions so you can eliminate the two that are most difficult. If, however, you are asked to answer all the questions, there may be danger in trying to answer the easiest one first because you may find that you will spend too much time on it. The best technique is to answer the first question, then proceed to the second, etc.

5) Time your answers. Before the exam begins, write down the time it started, then add the time allowed for the examination and write down the time it must be completed, then divide the time available somewhat as follows:
   - If 3-1/2 hours are allowed, that would be 210 minutes. If you have 80 objective-type questions, that would be an average of 2-1/2 minutes per question. Allow yourself no more than 2 minutes per question, or a total of 160 minutes, which will permit about 50 minutes to review.
   - If for the time allotment of 210 minutes there are 7 essay questions to answer, that would average about 30 minutes a question. Give yourself only 25 minutes per question so that you have about 35 minutes to review.

6) The most important instruction is to read each question and make sure you know what is wanted. The second most important instruction is to time yourself properly so that you answer every question. The third most important instruction is to answer every question. Guess if you have to but include something for each question. Remember that you will receive no credit for a blank and will probably receive some credit if you write something in answer to an essay question. If you guess a letter – say "B" for a multiple-choice question – you may have guessed right. If you leave a blank as an answer to a multiple-choice question, the examiners may respect your feelings but it will not add a point to your score. Some exams may penalize you for wrong answers, so in such cases only, you may not want to guess unless you have some basis for your answer.

7) Suggestions
   a. Objective-type questions
      1. Examine the question booklet for proper sequence of pages and questions
      2. Read all instructions carefully
      3. Skip any question which seems too difficult; return to it after all other questions have been answered
      4. Apportion your time properly; do not spend too much time on any single question or group of questions
      5. Note and underline key words – all, most, fewest, least, best, worst, same, opposite, etc.
      6. Pay particular attention to negatives
      7. Note unusual option, e.g., unduly long, short, complex, different or similar in content to the body of the question
      8. Observe the use of "hedging" words – probably, may, most likely, etc.

9. Make sure that your answer is put next to the same number as the question
10. Do not second-guess unless you have good reason to believe the second answer is definitely more correct
11. Cross out original answer if you decide another answer is more accurate; do not erase until you are ready to hand your paper in
12. Answer all questions; guess unless instructed otherwise
13. Leave time for review

b. Essay questions
1. Read each question carefully
2. Determine exactly what is wanted. Underline key words or phrases.
3. Decide on outline or paragraph answer
4. Include many different points and elements unless asked to develop any one or two points or elements
5. Show impartiality by giving pros and cons unless directed to select one side only
6. Make and write down any assumptions you find necessary to answer the questions
7. Watch your English, grammar, punctuation and choice of words
8. Time your answers; don't crowd material

8) Answering the essay question

Most essay questions can be answered by framing the specific response around several key words or ideas. Here are a few such key words or ideas:

M's: manpower, materials, methods, money, management
P's: purpose, program, policy, plan, procedure, practice, problems, pitfalls, personnel, public relations

a. Six basic steps in handling problems:
1. Preliminary plan and background development
2. Collect information, data and facts
3. Analyze and interpret information, data and facts
4. Analyze and develop solutions as well as make recommendations
5. Prepare report and sell recommendations
6. Install recommendations and follow up effectiveness

b. Pitfalls to avoid
1. Taking things for granted – A statement of the situation does not necessarily imply that each of the elements is necessarily true; for example, a complaint may be invalid and biased so that all that can be taken for granted is that a complaint has been registered
2. Considering only one side of a situation – Wherever possible, indicate several alternatives and then point out the reasons you selected the best one
3. Failing to indicate follow up – Whenever your answer indicates action on your part, make certain that you will take proper follow-up action to see how successful your recommendations, procedures or actions turn out to be
4. Taking too long in answering any single question – Remember to time your answers properly

EXAMINATION SECTION

EXAMINATION SECTION
TEST 1

DIRECTIONS: Each question or incomplete statement is followed by several suggested answers or completions. Select the one that *BEST* answers the question or completes the statement. *PRINT THE LETTER OF THE CORRECT ANSWER IN THE SPACE AT THE RIGHT.*

1. Which one of the following statements *BEST* describes the distinction between achievement and aptitude tests?
   The

   A. methods of measurement used in the two types of tests differ
   B. abilities measured by the two types of tests differ
   C. purposes for which the two types of tests are used differ
   D. content sampled by the two types of tests differs

   1.____

2. Of the following, the development of a blueprint for an achievement test is *MOST* closely related to

   A. criterion-centered validity
   B. content validity
   C. construct validity
   D. predictive validity

   2.____

3. Which one of the following types of scores is of *LEAST* value at the high school level?

   A. Grade scores   B. Percentile scores
   C. Standard scores   D. Stanines

   3.____

4. The best-controlled studies of the influence of genetic factors on human behavior are found in investigations of

   A. newborn babies   B. identical twins
   C. fraternal twins   D. siblings

   4.____

5. A vocational educator is planning a study in which machine operators with varying amounts of prior experiences (ranging from less than 1 year to more than 10 years) will be re-trained by two different methods. In this experiment, the amount of prior experience is called the

   A. independent variable B. dependent variable
   C. control variable   D. experimental variable

   5.____

6. Forms A and B of a 50 item test, each designed to be administered in 30 minutes, are combined into a single 100 item test and administered in a single hour-long sitting. In comparison to Form A or Form B, how variable and how reliable will the scores from the combined test be?

   A. More variable and more reliable
   B. More variable and less reliable
   C. Less variable and more reliable
   D. Less variable and less reliable

   6.____

1

7. Test specialists agree that most of the items on an achievement test should be of approximately 50 per cent difficulty. However, this principle need not be followed when one is constructing a test to measure

   A. ability to perform routine clerical tasks
   B. word knowledge
   C. reading comprehension
   D. ability to solve problems in arithmetic

8. In contemporary S-R theory, unverbalized "thoughts," "associations," and "images" are usually treated as

   A. insights
   B. mediators
   C. cognitions
   D. implicit linguistic responses

9. Which of the following BEST defines repression?

   A. Motivated forgetting
   B. Cognitive suppression
   C. Hysterical anxiety
   D. Reactive ambivalence

10. For systematic reviews of standardized tests, the BEST resource book is one edited by

    A. Thorndike
    B. Euros
    C. Ebel
    D. Cronbach

11. Which one of the following types of norms provides the CLOSEST approximation to equal units of measurement?

    A. Age norms
    B. Grade norms
    C. Percentile norms
    D. Standard scores

12. A test given to tenth grade students and compared with their present high school performance indicates what kind of validity?

    A. Predictive validity
    B. Content validity
    C. Construct validity
    D. Concurrent validity

13. The mean and the median of a frequency distribution of 200 scores are given as 65 and 75, respectively.
    This distribution is probably

    A. positively skewed
    B. negatively skewed
    C. normal
    D. bimodal

14. The Pearson-Product Moment formula is used to determine

    A. correlation
    B. reliability
    C. standard scores
    D. validity

15. The manual for a certain intelligence test contains tables for converting raw scores into both deviation IQ's and stanines. In discussing a pupil's performance on the test with his parent, it would be preferable to refer to the stanine rather than the IQ because the

    A. stanine is a more valid measure of intellectual ability than the IQ
    B. stanine is a more reliable measure of intellectual ability than the IQ
    C. IQ presents an appearance of precision measurement that is unwarranted
    D. concept of deviation IQ is too complex for the parent to grasp

15._____

16. If a test has a reliability coefficient of .80, what percentage of the observed scores may be attributed to errors of measurement?

    A. 20%   B. 36%   C. 64%   D. 80%

16._____

17. When a psychological disorder is described as "functional," it means that it is due to

    A. a chemical imbalance
    B. traumatic events in early childhood
    C. malfunctioning of the cerebral cortex
    D. unknown agents or causes

17._____

18. Which of the following psychologists is NOT identified with factor analysis?

    A. David Wechsler   B. L.L. Thurstone
    C. J.P. Guilford   D. PhillipVernon

18._____

19. In classical conditioning, extinction occurs when

    A. the conditioned stimulus is presented but not the unconditioned stimulus
    B. the unconditioned stimulus is presented but not the conditioned stimulus
    C. neither the conditioned nor the unconditioned stimuli are presented
    D. both the conditioned and unconditioned stimuli are presented

19._____

20. Thorndike is to "reward" as

    A. Hull is to "reinforcement"
    B. Lewin is to "orgone"
    C. Rogers is to "perception"
    D. Skinner is to "contiguity"

20._____

21. Which one of the following traits is of most importance in enabling an individual to maintain long-term leadership of a group?

    A. Empathy   B. Sympathy
    C. Selflessness   D. Egotism

21._____

22. An adolescent boy would like to have a girl friend. As an example of sublimation, he might

    A. proclaim himself a "woman-hater"
    B. withdraw from all inter-personal relationships
    C. convince himself that girls are really crazy about him
    D. begin to write romantic poetry

22._____

23. Jim studies all night before an examination in an attempt to learn the entire course. This is an example of

    A. distributed practice   B. massed practice
    C. practice effect   D. spread of effect

24. Terman's follow-up studies on a group of gifted children as compared to children of average intelligence revealed them to have

    A. better adjustment as shown on personality and character tests
    B. greater physical problems
    C. lower incomes
    D. more uneven academic achievement

25. One would expect the concept of "expectancy" to be emphasized by learning theorists who accept the point of view advanced by

    A. Lewin   B. Skinner
    C. Hull   D. Tolman

KEY (CORRECT ANSWERS)

1. C	11. D
2. B	12. D
3. A	13. B
4. B	14. A
5. A	15. C
6. A	16. A
7. A	17. D
8. B	18. A
9. A	19. A
10. B	20. A

21. A
22. D
23. B
24. A
25. D

TEST 2

DIRECTIONS: Each question or incomplete statement is followed by several suggested answers or completions. Select the one that BEST answers the question or completes the statement. PRINT THE LETTER OF THE CORRECT ANSWER IN THE SPACE AT THE RIGHT.

1. Billy wants to be admired, but he is too clumsy to achieve this goal through sports. Therefore, although not a bright pupil, he studies long hours and earns very high grades. This may be cited as an example of

    A. compensation
    B. projection
    C. rationalization
    D. reaction formation

    1._____

2. Of the following, the MOST important factor making for the development of friendship among young children is

    A. similarity in interests
    B. similarity in social class
    C. geographic proximity
    D. friendship among parents

    2._____

3. Harlow's work on mothering in monkeys suggests that the affective bond between the infant and the mother is based on

    A. feeding
    B. grooming
    C. tactile contact
    D. primitive vocalization

    3._____

4. What percent of the normal curve is found between plus and minus one standard deviation?

    A. 50   B. 68   C. 75   D. 84

    4._____

5. Which one of the following is the MOST important determinant of leadership among pre-adolescent boys?

    A. Intellectual ability
    B. Physical size and strength
    C. Popularity with girls
    D. Sensitivity to the needs of others

    5._____

6. Of the following, which statement concerning Thorndike's laws of learning would be considered most acceptable by contemporary psychologists? Thorndike's laws

    A. are applicable only to the learning of skills
    B. are applicable to the learning of the lower animals, but not to that of humans
    C. provide a description of the neuromuscular changes occurring during learning
    D. provide a description of factors that promote or hinder learning

    6._____

7. In Maslow's concept of a hierarchy of needs the highest level is

    A. self-esteem
    B. love and belongingness
    C. physiological needs
    D. self-actualization

    7._____

8. When a student complains that his low mark in a subject is due to the teacher's ineptitude, he is manifesting the defense mechanism of

    A. compensation
    B. displacement
    C. projection
    D. sublimation

9. Of the various body types described by Sheldon, the type that is associated with a generally introverted, restrained, and socially inhibited personality is the

    A. endomorph
    B. mesomorph
    C. gynandromorph
    D. ectomorph

10. The boy who is encouraged or required to be more independent at an earlier age tends to develop a/an

    A. low threshold for frustration
    B. inability to work well with others
    C. reluctance to accept adult authority
    D. strong need to achieve

11. The concept of "stages" in describing human development is LEAST applicable to

    A. Freud's psychoanalytic theory
    B. Piaget's cognitive theory
    C. Skinner's behavior theory
    D. Erikson's personality theory

12. The principal effect of nursery school attendance is upon the child's

    A. social development
    B. intellectual development
    C. perceptual development
    D. motor development

13. Which of the following terms is MOST clearly associated with stubborn reading disability?

    A. Apraxia
    B. Dysplasia
    C. Dyslexia
    D. Aphasia

14. The measure LEAST affected by extreme scores is the

    A. mean
    B. median
    C. range
    D. standard deviation

15. John is angry with his boss. However, he inhibits expressing hostility toward him. Later he reprimands his secretary. The defense mechanism used by John is

    A. compensation
    B. displacement
    C. projection
    D. reaction formation

16. Which author has recently revised the Goodenough Draw-A-Man Test?

    A. Bender
    B. Fernald
    C. Harris
    D. Harrower

17. Ebbinghaus conducted his experiments largely in the field of

    A. emotions
    B. memory
    C. motor control
    D. sensation

18. In an experiment, the ideal procedure for achieving pre-treatment equality of groups, within known statistical limits, is to assign subjects to groups

    A. by matching on all variables known to be relevant
    B. by matching on the basis of pre-test scores
    C. at random
    D. through a representative sampling process

19. The theory that the personality dimension of extroversion-introversion has a constitutional basis has been demonstrated by the research of

    A. Sheldon
    B. Jung
    C. Goldstein
    D. Eysenck

20. Latest studies of the physical basis of intelligence indicate that the foundations of consciousness and of attention are to be found in the

    A. hypothalamic region
    B. limbic system
    C. reticular formation
    D. cerebral cortex

21. The first psychological clinic in the United States was established in which of the following universities?

    A. Clark
    B. Stanford
    C. Columbia
    D. Pennsylvania

22. Attempts to provide systematic training to improve generalized aptitude for creative thinking and performance

    A. suggest that very little can be gained through such training
    B. have floundered because of inadequate techniques for training
    C. show great promise for the future
    D. are inconclusive because of lack of control groups

23. In which of the following situations would a classroom atmosphere of competitiveness be LEAST detrimental to the cultivation of interpersonal relationships? Classmates are

    A. unfamiliar with one another, but equal in abilities
    B. familiar with one another and equal in abilities
    C. unfamiliar with one another and greatly disparate in abilities
    D. familiar with one another and greatly disparate in abilities

24. On group intelligence tests Cyril Burt found the highest correlations between

    A. identical twins reared apart
    B. siblings reared together
    C. parents and own children living together
    D. identical twins reared together

25. The ultimate purpose of an achievement test is to
    A. ascertain current knowledge
    B. provide a baseline for curricula
    C. predict future behavior
    D. determine rate of learning

KEY (CORRECT ANSWERS)

1.	A	11.	C
2.	C	12.	A
3.	C	13.	C
4.	B	14.	B
5.	B	15.	B
6.	D	16.	C
7.	D	17.	B
8.	C	18.	C
9.	D	19.	D
10.	D	20.	C

21. D
22. C
23. B
24. D
25. C

TEST 3

DIRECTIONS: Each question or incomplete statement is followed by several suggested answers or completions. Select the one that BEST answers the question or completes the statement. PRINT THE LETTER OF THE CORRECT ANSWER IN THE SPACE AT THE RIGHT.

1. Pioneering studies in eliminating children's fears were conducted by Mary Cover Jones. The methods used, which are consistent with present-day learning theory, included all but one of the following:

    A. direct conditioning
    B. social imitation
    C. feeding responses
    D. systematic desensitization

2. In contrast to upward mobile adolescents, downward mobile adolescents are

    A. less ambivalent in self concept
    B. less interested in job security
    C. more confident in social relationships
    D. more dependent on their parents

3. In expounding his views on existential psychology, Allport directly criticized learning models in psychological theory because he felt they were

    A. incorrect
    B. too limited in scope
    C. irrelevant to contemporary life
    D. meaningful only in regard to animal behavior

4. In attempting to explain the direction of human conduct, the approach most closely identified with B.F. Skinner can be labelled

    A. cybernetic   B. reflex-arc
    C. tension-reduction   D. purposive

5. In the IOWA studies of children's reactions to frustration, which one of the following reactions was LEAST observed?

    A. Regression   B. Aggression
    C. Resignation   D. Accommodation

6. Maslow argues that destructive hostility is reactive rather than instinctive because

    A. uncovering therapy reduces it
    B. it is found in varying degrees in all people
    C. cross-cultural studies support this viewpoint
    D. self-actualizing persons show very little of it

7. Sheldon contends that there is a relationship between somatotype and personality characteristics. The weight of empirical evidence thus far

    A. tends to show negative relationships
    B. shows no relationship
    C. tends to support his hypothesis
    D. supports it for children but not for adults

9

8. Dick, who is 14 years old, has been given a curfew of midnight. Arriving home at 2:30 A.M., he explains his decision to come in late was based on the fact that everyone his age stays out that late. He is using

   A. compensation
   B. denial
   C. displacement
   D. rationalization

9. In order for a question or problem to provide a basis for psychological research, it must be

   A. free from any implied value judgments
   B. consistent with prior research findings
   C. stated in quantitative form
   D. answerable through some empirical procedure

10. In content validity, the term "content" most often refers to the

    A. duties of a particular job
    B. attitude of the individual taking a test
    C. objectives of a unit of instruction
    D. traits necessary for academic or vocational success

11. The use of statistics computed on samples to make generalizations about population parameters is known as statistical

    A. description
    B. extrapolation
    C. inference
    D. sampling

12. In a normal distribution, if the mean equals 100, then the

    A. median and mode must equal 100
    B. median must equal 100 but the mode may not equal 100
    C. mode must equal 100 but the median may not equal 100
    D. mode and median may not equal 100

13. Of the following, the most significant trend in intelligence testing in recent years is the measurement of

    A. a composite of many abilities
    B. motor abilities mainly
    C. practical judgment in social situations
    D. several types of mental abilities independently

14. In a normal distribution the 84th percentile corresponds to a T score of

    A. 70   B. 60   C. 50   D. 40

15. On a test of social studies, Bill answered 40 items correctly out of the 50 on the test. From this information, we know that Bill

    A. is at the 80th percentile
    B. is well informed in social studies
    C. failed to answer correctly 20% of the items
    D. is above the average for his grade

16. Thorndike's early formulation of the law of effect 16.____

    A. was little more than a formalization of common observations
    B. anticipated the reinforcement principle adopted in many conditioned response theories
    C. maintained that behavior must be mediated by conscious ideas or awareness
    D. stressed the Importance of satisfiers relative to annoyers

17. Mr. Brown maintains that "every time I construct a test, I make sure that only very few students will have time to complete every item." Mr. Brown's approach is 17.____

    A. good, because he will discriminate between his poorer and his better students more easily
    B. poor, because most of his students will no longer have a goal of 100 per cent to strive for
    C. good, because speed and accuracy are highly correlated in most areas of instruction
    D. poor, because speed of response is rarely a primary goal of instruction

18. Which one of the following generalizations can properly be drawn from the research literature dealing with test administration? 18.____

    A. It is best to schedule examinations in the mid-morning, early in the week
    B. It is best to schedule examinations in the mid-morning, late in the week
    C. It is best to schedule examinations in the mid-morning, in the middle of the week
    D. There is no evidence supporting any preference for any hour or day for scheduling examinations

19. When test-retest reliability data are reported in a test manual, providing data for a very heterogeneous sample will have what effect on the reliability coefficient? It will be 19.____

    A. too low
    B. too high
    C. the same as for a homogeneous sample
    D. not significant if the sample is large

20. Of the following, the most serious limitation of observational methods of evaluating personal-social adjustment is that 20.____

    A. effective observation demands clinically trained observers
    B. observer bias tends to color the observational process
    C. meaningful observation requires cooperation by the subject
    D. interpretation of the findings calls for extensive knowledge of the subject's background

21. Studies of the correlation between IQ and school success generally yield coefficients of .60 on the elementary school level and coefficients of .40 on the college level. This is due to the fact that elementary school children, as compared to college students, are 21.____

    A. younger
    B. more evenly divided in terms of sex groups
    C. more highly motivated towards school success
    D. more variable in terms of intelligence

22. Which of the following is the minimum age for which the Wechsler Preschool and Primary Scale of Intelligence is designed?   22.___

    A. Two   B. Three   C. Four   D. Five

23. Among the following, the chief source for finding reviews of recent books in the field of psychology is   23.___

    A. Psychological Review
    B. Psychological Science
    C. Contemporary Psychology
    D. American Psychologist

24. A group of judges has been asked to rank 10 candidates for a position in order of preference. Each judge is asked to use a paired-comparison approach in order to arrive at the relative ranks he assigns to the candidates. In comparison to other ranking procedures, the paired-comparison approach generally is more   24.___

    A. valid
    B. reliable
    C. discriminating among the better candidates
    D. discriminating among the poorer candidates

25. The major problem in using the paired-comparison technique for developing attitude scales is that the   25.___

    A. reliability of the scales cannot be determined
    B. scale values assigned to successive statements do not differ by equal amounts
    C. attitude of a truly neutral person cannot be determined accurately
    D. process is too time-consuming

KEY (CORRECT ANSWERS)

1. D		11. C	
2. D		12. A	
3. B		13. D	
4. B		14. B	
5. D		15. C	
6. A		16. B	
7. C		17. D	
8. D		18. D	
9. D		19. B	
10. C		20. B	

21. D
22. C
23. C
24. B
25. D

TEST 4

DIRECTIONS: Each question or incomplete statement is followed by several suggested answers or completions. Select the one that BEST answers the question or completes the statement. PRINT THE LETTER OF THE CORRECT ANSWER IN THE SPACE AT THE RIGHT.

1. In which one of the following measurement situations would the use of a standardized product scale be most appropriate? When measuring the

    A. workmanship of a bench made in the woodworking shop
    B. quality of a poster made by a commercial artist
    C. quality of an individual's handwriting
    D. ability of an individual to spell a list of words

    1._____

2. Some standardized tests convert the raw scores obtained by pupils into grade scores; others convert raw scores into percentile ranks. Which one of the following BEST describes the advantage in the latter procedure?

    A. It is easier to convert percentile ranks into per cent marks
    B. Percentile ranks tend to be more reliable than grade scores
    C. Use of grade scores implies common pupil experiences; use of percentile ranks does not
    D. Differences between percentile ranks reflect equal units of ability

    2._____

3. With regard to the reinforcing effect of changes in level of stimulation, recent findings indicate that

    A. only a decrease in stimulation is reinforcing
    B. only an increase in stimulation is reinforcing
    C. neither an increase or a decrease in stimulation is reinforcing
    D. either an increase or a decrease may be reinforcing

    3._____

4. Factor analysis is a technique that may be applied to a group of tests in order to identify a small number of underlying factors that can account for the

    A. differences in mean scores on the different tests
    B. intercorrelations among the tests
    C. valid variance in the entire test pool
    D. homogeneous content in the tests

    4._____

5. Which of the following is the most important step in preparing an animal for learning experiments?

    A. Acculturation to the apparatus
    B. Deprivation of food
    C. Exposure to negative stimuli
    D. Development of confidence in the experimenter

    5._____

6. Studies of anxiety and its effect on learning generally support the following conclusion about high-anxiety subjects. They do

    A. equally well on simple and complex tasks
    B. well or poorly, unpredictably, on simple and complex tasks
    C. poorly on simple tasks, but do well on complex tasks
    D. well on simple tasks, but do poorly on complex tasks

    6._____

13

7. The correlation between the scores obtained by a group of 20 subjects on Test A and Test B is computed. To determine whether the obtained *r* is significant, under what *df* value should one enter the appropriate table?

   A. 18   B. 20   C. 38   D. 40

8. To increase the reliability of a 15-item rating scale, the most effective procedure would be to

   A. increase the number of items on the scale
   B. increase the number of persons to be rated
   C. pool the ratings given by several independent judges
   D. eliminate ratings that are very deviant

9. When do coordination and convergence of the eyes begin to develop in the infant?

   A. Immediately after birth
   B. After one week
   C. After two weeks
   D. After three weeks

10. In the WISC, the subtest which shows the lowest correlation with other valid tests of intelligence is

    A. block designs   B. comprehension
    C. digit span   D. similarities

11. By virtue of his earlier interaction with his mother, a child may display affectional responses to other adults. This is an example of

    A. secondary reinforcement
    B. stimulus generalization
    C. response diffusion
    D. learned mediation

12. Regarding the role of reward in learning, a controversy in the psychological literature still exists between

    A. reinforcement theorists and contiguity theorists
    B. operant theorists and behavior theorists
    C. cognitive theorists and field theorists
    D. psychoanalytic theorists and psycholinguistic theorists

13. Habitual responses that have been acquired under conditions of aperiodic reinforcement tend to

    A. fluctuate erratically   B. extinguish slowly
    C. extinguish quickly   D. generalize widely

14. With repeated practice on a series of similar problems, it is frequently found that organisms require fewer and fewer trials to learn. This is an example of

    A. cue integration   B. learning set
    C. response facilitation   D. error suppression

15. Statistics on the incidence of mental disorders indicate that, in the last 80 years, the rate of psychosis has

    A. tripled
    B. doubled
    C. remained stable
    D. decreased slightly

16. Studies of sensory deprivation during infancy indicate that lack of stimulation during this period is most likely to result in

    A. low frustration tolerance
    B. poor psychomotor coordination
    C. lack of emotional responsiveness
    D. retarded intellectual development

17. Which one of the following BEST illustrates the distinction between "performance" and "competence" as drawn by contemporary psycholinguists?

    A. A child can vocalize before he can speak
    B. A child's motor development depends upon language acquisition
    C. A child is more limited in language production than in language comprehension
    D. A child acquires language to meet his need to function as an effective person

18. In the United States, the standard diagnostic system for classifying mental disorders is the American Psychiatric Association's

    A. "Diagnostic and Statistical Manual of Mental Disorders"
    B. "Standard System of Neurotic and Psychotic Conditions"
    C. "Taxonomy of Mental Pathologies"
    D. "Identifying and Classifying Diseases of the Mind"

19. An 8 year old pupil is told by his teacher that he cannot join his group in play because he needs to practice writing. The boy starts crying, drops to the floor, sobs heavily and strikes the floor with hands and legs. The behavior exhibited by the boy is an example of

    A. repression
    B. identification
    C. aggression
    D. regression

20. At the present time, the most comprehensive analysis of educational goals is to be found in

    A. the summary report of the Eight Year Study of Progressive Education
    B. the publications of the Educational Policies Commission
    C. John Dewey's Human Nature and Conduct and Experience and Education
    D. the Taxonomy of Educational Objectives

21. Bruner and Page, among others, contend that children can learn anything that adults can. Ausubel, in his writings,

    A. extends the contention
    B. modifies the contention
    C. rejects the contention
    D. supports the contention

22. When stimuli are perceived as emotional, they will

    A. dominate the learning process
    B. influence the learning process
    C. disrupt the learning process
    D. control the learning process

23. Within the context of Hullian drive theory, reinforcement is assumed to be a consequence of

    A. drive reduction
    B. cue clarification
    C. stimulus substitution
    D. task completion

24. A psychotic child taking the WISC might be expected to have

    A. higher performance than verbal test scores
    B. lower performance than verbal test scores
    C. extremely low verbal and performance ratings
    D. relatively even verbal and performance ratings

25. On the Stanford-Binet, 68.3 percent of the IQ's would fall between

    A. 50 - 75
    B. 120 - 140
    C. 84 - 116
    D. 90 - 110

KEY (CORRECT ANSWERS)

1.	C	11.	B
2.	C	12.	A
3.	D	13.	B
4.	B	14.	B
5.	B	15.	C
6.	D	16.	D
7.	A	17.	C
8.	C	18.	A
9.	A	19.	D
10.	C	20.	D

21. C
22. B
23. A
24. B
25. C

TEST 5

DIRECTIONS: Each question or incomplete statement is followed by several suggested answers or completions. Select the one that *BEST* answers the question or completes the statement. *PRINT THE LETTER OF THE CORRECT ANSWER IN THE SPACE AT THE RIGHT.*

1. In reference to learning, most children will tend to set goals for themselves which are   1._____

   A. similar to those of their peers
   B. different from those of their peers
   C. too difficult or complex
   D. too easy or too low

2. Jerome Bruner's description of the changing concept of transfer of training in learning emphasizes   2._____

   A. mastery of facts and techniques
   B. teaching and learning materials
   C. teaching and learning of structure
   D. mastery of the humanities

3. Studies of the characteristics of brain-injured children have produced contradictory results. Which one of the following *most likely* accounts for these results?   3._____

   A. Failure to use control groups
   B. Lack of homogeneity in site and extent of lesion
   C. Conflicting theories of etiology
   D. Faulty experimental methodology

4. Among environmental influences upon the development of intelligence socioeconomic level has been subjected to the greatest amount of investigation. Greatest progress in achieving less ambiguous conclusions would *most probably* result from   4._____

   A. more adequate sampling procedures
   B. developing culture-fair tests
   C. more refined statistical analyses
   D. better specification of variables

5. Guilford described divergent thinking as equated with   5._____

   A. creativity   B. logical thinking
   C. memory   D. recognition

6. Analysis of the factorial structure of the WISC leads to which of the following result? It   6._____

   A. provides a reliable basis for interpreting subtest scores
   B. suggests that subtests measure different aspects of intelligence at different age levels
   C. supports the theory of intelligence upon which the WISC is predicated
   D. supports the common practice of assigning equal weights to subtests at all age levels

17

7. Comparison of the 1960 Stanford-Binet with the WISC verbal IQ has shown that, at the superior level,

   A. SB produces higher IQ's
   B. SB and WISC produce similar IQ's
   C. WISC produces higher IQ's
   D. the results are inconclusive

8. Children involved in initial learning tend to do significantly better on problems where the rule or principle is

   A. given or stated
   B. independently derived
   C. minimized
   D. neglected

9. A learning program based on classical behaviorism would stress

   A. conditioning
   B. thinking
   C. understanding
   D. volitional activity

10. The view of neurotogenesis which includes as a basic construct that "basic early experiences accumulate to establish in each individual a central emotional position to which the personality returns automatically from any excursion to other emotional states" is associated with

    A. Karen Horney
    B. Lawrence Kubie
    C. Wilhelm Reich
    D. Erich Fromm

11. In the eye, the function of the lens is to

    A. constrict and dilate the pupil
    B. focus light on the retina
    C. permit light to enter
    D. regulate the amount of light

12. Which of the following represents the major change in in the 1960 Stanford-Binet from the 1937 revision?

    A. Abandonment of the ratio IQ
    B. Development of performance and verbal IQ's
    C. Inclusion of tests for three year olds
    D. Restandardization on school age children

13. The null hypothesis

    A. is supported by a critical ratio that is near zero
    B. assumes that no difference exists between the two populations that are being sampled
    C. lies in the center of the given confidence limits
    D. states that none of the hypotheses being tested is correct

14. Difference scores, obtained by subtracting one score from another, tend to be MOST reliable when the two scores are

    A. highly valid as separate measures
    B. expressed in the same units
    C. uncorrelated with one another
    D. individually unreliable

15. To correct a correlation coefficient for attenuation is to eliminate statistically the effect of the

    A. sampling variability of the correlation coefficient
    B. non-homogeneity of the trait universe
    C. standard error of estimate
    D. unreliability of either or both variables

16. A gamble thinks that wishing hard for a seven will affect what number comes up when he throws the dice.
    He believes in

    A. precognition   B. clairvoyance
    C. telepathy   D. psychokinesis

17. What is the z score equivalent of a raw score of 40 when the mean = 30 and the standard deviation = 8?

    A. z = +10.00   B. z = +8.00
    C. z = +5.00   D. z = +1.25

18. An investigator is studying the relationship between two traits A and B. He finds a correlation of .50 and describes it as significant at the .01 level.
    This means that he

    A. rejects the hypothesis r = .00
    B. rejects the hypothesis r = .50
    C. accepts the hypothesis r = .00
    D. accepts the hypothesis r = .50

19. Of the following, which is most in agreement with recent research on dreams?

    A. Most dreams last from several minutes to more than one hour
    B. Most people dream; a few do not
    C. Dreams occur usually during NREM sleep
    D. Dreams of sleep walkers usually resemble what they did while walking about during the day

20. Which of the questions below deals with the *INTERNAL* validity of an experiment?

    A. Have statistically significant results been obtained?
    B. Do the experimental results support the experimental hypothesis?
    C. Were appropriate statistical techniques used to analyze the experimental data?
    D. Did the experimental treatments make a difference in this specific experiment?

Questions 21-24.

Questions 21 through 24 are based on the following case description:

Prank was referred for study because he was considered to be restless, inattentive, talkative, and a disturbing influence in the classroom. Psychometric data are as follows: present grade 5.2; C.A. 10-8; Stanford-Binet, Form L. M.A. 14-6; I.Q. 140; Achievement grade levels - Reading Comprehension 8.7, Spelling 7.9, Arithmetic Computation 7.6, Arithmetic Reasoning 8.8.

21. Assuming continued normal development is is MOST probable that he

    A. will be a very superior student in high school and a superior student in college
    B. will be a superior student in high school and an average student in college
    C. should be considered a potential genius
    D. will be more successful as an engineer or scientist than as a lawyer or physician

22. Of the following tentative hypotheses, the one which is the MOST probable explanation of his classroom behavior is that he

    A. has been badly spoiled at home
    B. suffers from hyperthyroidism
    C. is a case of primary behavior disorder
    D. is not sufficiently challenged by the classroom work

23. The psychologist is probably justified in recommending to Frank's present teacher that

    A. he appoint a committee of three pupils to recommend to the class how they should treat Frank
    B. his conduct should be accepted without adverse comment
    C. Frank should assist the teacher by reporting instances of misbehavior by other members of the class
    D. Frank should be permitted to assume special study assignments

24. Frank's mother complains that none of his teachers has understood or appreciated him. She says he is a model child at home and refuses to believe that he misbehaves in school. The psychologist is justified in

    A. accepting her statements at face value
    B. suspecting that Prank is overindulged at home
    C. encouraging her to place him in a private school where he will be appreciated
    D. telling her that she has been guilty of spoiling him very badly

25. The average Accomplishment Quotient for children with I.Q.'s of 120 or more has been found to be

    A. below 100   B. at 100
    C. approximately 110   D. at 120 or above

KEY (CORRECT ANSWERS)

1. A
2. C
3. B
4. D
5. A

6. B
7. A
8. A
9. A
10. B

11. B
12. A
13. B
14. C
15. D

16. D
17. D
18. A
19. A
20. D

21. A
22. D
23. D
24. B
25. A

EXAMINATION SECTION
TEST 1

DIRECTIONS: Each question or incomplete statement is followed by several suggested answers or completions. Select the one that BEST answers the question or completes the statement. *PRINT THE LETTER OF THE CORRECT ANSWER IN THE SPACE AT THE RIGHT.*

1. The reliabilities of the individual subtests of the Wechsler Intelligence Scale for Children are

   A. lower at age 7 1/2 than at age 10 1/2
   B. lower at age 10 1/2 than at age 7 1/2
   C. approximately equal to the reliability of the verbal scale
   D. approximately equal to the reliability of the performance scale

2. If the Standard Error of Estimate of a test is 6, an obtained score will probably not vary on retest more than 6 points

   A. 32% of the time   B. 22% of the time
   C. 68% of the time   D. 88% of the time

3. An example of negative correlation is the relationship between

   A. reliability and standard error of measurement
   B. variability and standard deviation
   C. IQ and percentile rank
   D. validity and predictability

4. Most empirical studies indicate a correlation of about .75 between the Stanford-Binet and the Wechsler Intelligence Scale for Children. This indicates that

   A. the WISC is less reliable than the Stanford-Binet
   B. only 75% of the WISC I.Q.'s will agree with the Stanford-Binet I.Q.'s
   C. the confidence limits of the WISC I.Q.'s are computed with 25% error
   D. approximately 50% of the variability between the two tests is statistically independent

5. The reliability coefficients of most standardized intelligence tests when compared with the validity coefficients of the same test are generally

   A. significantly higher
   B. significantly lower
   C. approximately equal
   D. either higher or lower depending on the test

6. Among the following, the HIGHEST correlation between school marks and IQ's for groups of individuals will most probably be found in

   A. elementary school   B. high school
   C. college   D. graduate school

7. A recent research study conducted in a small town school reported a correlation of .85 between 5th grade IQ's and scholastic averages. An objective conclusion is:

   A. For this class, level of achievement is determined largely by level of intelligence.
   B. For this class, no inferences can be made regarding the effect of intelligence upon level of achievement.
   C. Basic errors in statistical computation were probably made.
   D. The design of the study was probably inappropriate.

8. Mr. Jones, the principal of a public school, discovers that the children in the fifth grade fall below the national norms for their grade in arithmetic. The psychologist should suggest that

   A. he promptly organize special remedial help in class so that they may reach the norm for their grades
   B. he explain to the teachers that they must motivate the children more constructively so as to improve their work
   C. he promptly organize a program of individual remedial help
   D. none of the above

9. Mrs. Johnson, the principal of the school, asks Mr. Kramer, the psychologist, to inform one of the teachers that she is relieving her of her assignment as guidance counselor. Of the following, the MOST appropriate action the psychologist can take is to

   A. suggest to the principal that she handle this matter herself
   B. point out to the principal that for the psychologist
   C. to do so would impair his relationship with the teacher
   D. write a note to the teacher informing her of the action that was taken
   E. discuss the decision with the teacher

10. Mr. Wilson is one of the most popular teachers in the school. He is friendly and soft-spoken. In school he helps children solve their grievances by putting on boxing gloves. In his leisure time he watches wrestling and boxing matches. His favorite programs are murder mysteries and westerns. This description would lead us to the conclusion that Mr. Wilson is MOST probably

    A. basically a passive person
    B. sublimating some of his aggressive drives
    C. experiencing constant frustration
    D. needs psychotherapy

11. Mr. Anderson, a teacher in the school, stops the psychologist who is passing through the hall and points to a boy standing near him. He describes in angry tones how the child struck a girl in the class. He asks him to see the boy to "straighten him out." Of the following the MOST appropriate action for the psychologist to take is to

    A. schedule an early date for psychological testing
    B. discuss with the teacher possible causes of the child's behavior
    C. suggest to the teacher methods of attaining effective discipline in class
    D. point out the effect of the lack of the teacher's objectivity on the child's adjustment

12. If a two-year-old child exhibited temper tantrums, the MOST probable explanation of this behavior would be that he is

    A. reacting to the birth of a sibling
    B. reacting in a fashion appropriate to his stage of development
    C. overindulged by his parents, but inconsistently disciplined
    D. reacting to a disturbed family situation

13. Robert, age 8, lives with his mother who is separated from her husband. According to the health card no action was taken by the parent in obtaining the recommended glasses and urgent dental work for Robert. Robert frequently comes to school without breakfast and both his face and clothing are dirty. Because he stays out late at night, he falls asleep in class. Of the following, the BEST referral resource to use would be the

    A. Family Service Society
    B. Society for Prevention of Cruelty to Children
    C. Juvenile Aid Bureau
    D. Children's Aid Society

14. The "Directory of Social Agencies of the City of New York" is a publication which is prepared by the

    A. Welfare Council
    B. Department of Welfare
    C. Department of Mental Hygiene
    D. New School for Social Research

15. Malcolm, age 4, gave no human movement responses on the Rorschach. For Malcolm, this is indicative of

    A. sub-normal intelligence
    B. emotional constriction
    C. inadequate ego development
    D. none of the above

16. Epilepsy is mainly associated with

    A. brain injury
    B. migraine
    C. dysrythmia
    D. aggressivity

17. A disturbance of language perception and expression is called

    A. aphasia   B. amnesia   C. amentia   D. alexia

18. Alcoholism is MOST commonly connected with

    A. dysrythmia
    B. neurosis
    C. psychopathy
    D. overt homosexuality

19. The polygraph is MOST useful for diagnosing

    A. epilepsy
    B. aggressivity
    C. deception
    D. brain damage

20. The electroencephalogram is MOST useful for diagnosing

    A. brain tumor
    B. epilepsy
    C. brain injury
    D. mental deficiency

21. Shock therapy is MOST likely to be recommended for

    A. paranoid schizophrenics
    B. depressed psychotics
    C. severe psychoneurotics
    D. psychopaths

22. Prefrontal lobotomy is MOST likely to be recommended for

    A. aggressive psychotics
    B. apathetic psychotics
    C. paranoid psychotics
    D. psychopaths

23. Most authorities believe that mental deficiency is

    A. never hereditary
    B. always hereditary
    C. sometimes hereditary
    D. rarely hereditary

24. Recent experiments utilizing glutamic acid in an attempt to raise the intellectual level of retarded children have resulted in

    A. inconclusive findings
    B. a marked temporary rise in intellectual level
    C. a marked permanent rise in intellectual level
    D. a slight temporary decline in intellectual level

25. An individual's Rorschach protocol may be MOST profitably interpreted in the light of

    A. his behavior while being tested
    B. his case history
    C. his other test results
    D. his presenting problems

26. The Kuder Preference Record tests

    A. attitudes
    B. interests
    C. aptitudes
    D. achievement

27. Personality inventories are LEAST likely to be useful for testing

    A. job applicants
    B. college applicants
    C. military personnel
    D. neuropsychiatric patients

28. In the construction of tests, it is EASIEST to assure oneself of the test's

    A. validity
    B. reliability
    C. objectivity
    D. interpretability

29. If a child's score on a group intelligence test is less than 1 PE (probable error) from the mean score, this score

   A. is not reliable since it is low
   B. is improbable or fallacious
   C. cannot be converted into a percentile score
   D. lies within the middle 50% of the group

30. A report states that a child received a percentile rank of 11. This means that the child was able to

   A. get 11% of the answers correct
   B. get 89% of the answers correct
   C. surpass 11% of the population with which he was compared
   D. surpass 89% of the population with which he was compared

31. In general, correlations between different verbal group intelligence test IQ's of pupils in a given grade may be expected to fall within the range of

   A. .90 - 1.00   B. .70 - .90
   C. .40 - .70   D. .20 - .40

32. Of the following aspects of intelligence, the one which is measured most INADEQUATELY by present group intelligence tests is

   A. creative imagination
   B. insight into logical relationships
   C. verbal comprehension
   D. mathematical reasoning

33. The chief DISADVANTAGE of teacher-prepared tests is that they

   A. are not sufficiently objective
   B. are too difficult for the average teacher to prepare
   C. lack adequate standardization for grouping purposes within the class
   D. fail to provide a basis for comparison with children in other schools and classes

34. If it were desirable to convert a pupil's intelligence, reading and arithmetic test scores for the purpose of direct comparison, we would need to know for each test the

   A. percentile rank   B. standard deviation
   C. standard error   D. interquartile range

35. Lionel obtains a grade score of 2.7 on a valid standardized arithmetic test which you administer. His IQ based on the Binet is 72. In order to approximate whether he is working at capacity in arithmetic you must also know

   A. the range of scores for the class
   B. his chronological age
   C. the mean scores for the class
   D. the reliability of the test

36. If an unselected group of children is examined with the Binet at ages 3, 8 and 13, then the correlations between the IQ's obtained may be expected to be

   A. highest between ages 8 and 13
   B. highest between ages 3 and 8
   C. highest between ages 3 and 13
   D. closely equivalent for all of the above ages

37. According to Strauss, the teacher of a brain injured child should provide

   A. the child with many opportunities for practicing fine motor coordination
   B. a variety of brightly colored illustrations to motivate the child's reading
   C. for frequent isolation of the child from other pupils in the classroom and for special activity
   D. longer than usual work periods before she suggests a change of task to the child

38. To measure a subject's ability for abstract thinking, the BEST of the following four tests is the

   A. Wechsler-Bellevue
   B. Rorschach
   C. Babcock
   D. Goldstein-Scheerer

39. The MAJOR weakness of projective tests is that

   A. they are too intuitive
   B. they fail to produce consistent findings among different psychologists
   C. their interpretation involves too much projection of the examiner
   D. their validity has not been adequately established

40. Research on child development and adjustment has been MOST severely challenged by the problem of

   A. selecting appropriate statistical methods
   B. predicting future behavior
   C. confirming studies
   D. deriving broad conclusions

41. If a child is mentally retarded, his academic potential can be explained MOST readily to his parent in terms of the status of other children

   A. in his class
   B. of similar CA
   C. of similar MA
   D. of similar IQ

42. It is MOST probable that a school-age child characterized, on the basis of psychological tests, as a mental defective might, in fact, be

   A. epileptic   B. deaf   C. mute   D. schizophrenic

43. The classroom behavior MOST characteristic of the brain injured child includes

   A. distractibility, hyperactivity and lack of inhibition
   B. listlessness, withdrawal and compulsiveness
   C. aggressiveness, fearfulness and egocentrism
   D. perseveration, fatigue and apathy

44. An indispensable condition for effective remedial instruction in reading is

   A. appropriate teaching material
   B. selection of correct teaching methods
   C. frequent regular contacts with the child
   D. proper motivation of the child

45. In oral reading, mixed lateral dominance is MOST often associated with

   A. omissions
   B. substitutions
   C. repetitions
   D. reversals

46. A child's MOST rapid rate of mental growth generally occurs

   A. during the first few months of life
   B. between the ages of 3 - 6
   C. between the ages of 6 - 12
   D. during early adolescence

47. A psychopath may be distinguished by the fact that he commits antisocial acts

   A. consistently
   B. without customary reaction to guilt
   C. without awareness of what he is doing
   D. violently

48. Of the following techniques, the one which is considered to be characteristic of non-directive or client-centered therapy is

   A. encouraging transference
   B. reflection of feeling
   C. free association
   D. permissive questioning

49. Psychoanalytic writers consider the MOST important aspect of an analyst's training to be

   A. his training in psychoanalytic concepts
   B. his training in medicine
   C. his training in analysis
   D. his general psychological training

50. In the transference situation, it is MOST probable that there will be

   A. positive feeling between analyst and patient
   B. negative feeling between analyst and patient
   C. neutral feeling between analyst and patient
   D. positive and negative feelings between, analyst and patient

KEY (CORRECT ANSWERS)

1. A	11. B	21. B	31. B	41. C
2. A	12. B	22. A	32. A	42. D
3. A	13. B	23. C	33. D	43. A
4. D	14. A	24. A	34. B	44. D
5. A	15. D	25. B	35. B	45. D
6. A	16. C	26. B	36. A	46. A
7. B	17. A	27. D	37. C	47. B
8. D	18. B	28. C	38. D	48. B
9. B	19. C	29. D	39. D	49. C
10. B	20. B	30. C	40. B	50. D

TEST 2

DIRECTIONS: Each question or incomplete statement is followed by several suggested answers or completions. Select the one that BEST answers the question or completes the statement. *PRINT THE LETTER OF THE CORRECT ANSWER IN THE SPACE AT THE RIGHT.*

Questions 1-50.

1. In the first months of an infant's life, the baby's reflex responses are

    A. almost the only reactions the baby shows
    B. virtually absent from behavior
    C. more accurate than later in life
    D. less conspicuous than generalized mass reactions

2. Play and reading interests of boys and girls will be found to be most different at the age of

    A. three years
    B. six years
    C. twelve years
    D. eighteen years

3. The unsociability often reported for very bright children is *most likely* to be due to

    A. their biological makeup
    B. their complete absorption in intellectual pursuits
    C. their lack of personal attractiveness
    D. the absence of suitable companions

4. If we measure a number of individuals upon a variety of complex mental functions, we will find that the different functions show

    A. a negative relationship
    B. no relationship
    C. a fairly high degree of positive relationship
    D. practically a perfect positive relationship

5. As children in groups with very limited environments, such as canal-boat dwellers, "hollow-folk," etc., grow older, their I.Q. is found to

    A. increase
    B. stay the same
    C. decrease
    D. vary widely and irregularly

6. Which of the following BEST characterizes Hildreth's BIBLIOGRAPHY OF TESTS AND RATING SCALES (together with its supplement)?

    A. Full description of each test listed
    B. Critical comments on each test listed
    C. Virtually complete listing of all tests and scales
    D. All of the above

7. Forgetting curves are characterized by

    A. a more rapid initial drop followed by slower forgetting
    B. a constant rate of loss
    C. a slow drop at first, with more rapid loss
    D. none of these

8. Formulation of rules, definitions, and verbal generalizations

   A. has virtually no place in the process of learning
   B. should be the final outcome of learning
   C. should accompany and be accompanied by actual experience
   D. should be the first step in any learning

9. Transfer from one subject to another or to life situations will be increased if

   A. techniques and applications are emphasized
   B. the first subject is very difficult
   C. a good deal of drill is given in the first subject
   D. the situations seem quite different

10. Of the following general statements about deterioration in mental patients, which is the MOST questionable at present?

    A. More recently acquired forms of reaction are lost before those formed earlier in life.
    B. Generalization and abstraction in psychoses is qualitatively the same as that in the young child.
    C. Deterioration in many cases regarded as hopeless appears to be reversible.
    D. The responses of a deteriorated person show generally a definite patterning which tends to mask his defects.

11. Concerning the course of intellectual deterioration in the mental disorders, it is CORRECT to state that

    A. defect in the ability to generalize is more characteristic of schizophrenia than of other psychotic states
    B. concept formation deteriorates more slowly in schizophrenia than in senile psychosis
    C. decreased speed and persistence in mental activity are characteristic of epilepsy
    D. senile patients suffer more impairment in the recall of long past events than in recent memory

12. According to mental test comparisons of cooperative patients in the various disease groups, the group which shows the LEAST intellectual impairment is

    A. paranoid schizophrenia
    B. psychopathic personality
    C. hebephrenic schizophrenia
    D. hysteria

13. Schizophrenic speech is BEST characterized by

    A. loose, approximate use of words and reaction to superficial similarities among ideas and objects
    B. loose, approximate use of words and failure to make use of similarities or analogies
    C. unusual amount of stammering and reaction to superficial similarities among ideas and objects
    D. unusual amount of stammering and failure to make use of similarities or analogies

14. It is the central, distinguishing feature of the depressive phase of manic-depressive psychosis that

    A. the patient is keenly aware of lacking a motive for existence
    B. the patient attaches his depression to some irrelevant or imaginary cause
    C. the patient is excessively disturbed over some recent trouble
    D. the patient is overactive, restless, and even agitated

15. According to the Doctrine of Formal Discipline, the study of Latin is valuable because

    A. an educated individual should know Latin
    B. the study of a difficult subject strengthens the intellect in general
    C. many English words come from Latin
    D. Latin helps with other college subjects

16. According to studies reported by Edward L. Thorndike, ability to learn

    A. is greatest in early childhood
    B. increases throughout life
    C. reaches a maximum in the thirtees and then drops rapidly
    D. reaches a maximum in the twenties and then drops slowly

17. Problem-solving behavior, according to the views of E.L. Thorndike,

    A. first makes its appearance at adolescence
    B. first makes its appearance at the age of about 10 years and grows rapidly from then to adolescence
    C. is present in rudimentary form in pre-school children and develops gradually throughout the whole school career
    D. is clearly evident in superior children at birth

18. In which of the following abilities do dull and gifted children tend to differ most markedly?

    A. Arithmetical computation
    B. Drawing
    C. Reading comprehension
    D. Spelling

19. Which of the following statements reflects an attitude concerning anecdotal records that would be soundest to take?

    A. Even if not entirely accurate, anecdotal records reveal how his teachers probably perceive a pupil.
    B. Such records are useful only when limited to unbiased reports of overt behavior as recorded by trained specialists.
    C. Despite their limitations, anecdotal records are more valid than any other method of appraising personality.
    D. Anecdotal records are bound to be unreliable because teachers are biased favorably or otherwise according to how well a pupil behaves.

20. Regardless of one's standpoint, it is generally desirable in a series of counseling interviews for the counselor to

   A. structure with the client in advance the topics to be discussed
   B. structure the interviews as one goes along
   C. prevent the client from structuring the interview
   D. avoid structuring the interview on one's own part

21. A high school senior with a good record in mathematics has been referred to the school psychologist because of a drop in his grades. When asked for his opinion as to why his math grades have deteriorated, he complains that his math teacher doesn't explain the work and that when the student does poorly on a test, she says he should be able to do better, but doesn't help him. The school psychologist should

   A. recommend a transfer to another mathematics class
   B. suggest to the teacher that she consider whether the use of concrete materials would not increase student comprehension
   C. discuss the student's complaint with the chairman of the mathematics department
   D. do none of the above

22. Which of the following represents the LEAST valuable use to which a school psychologist can put a case conference to which have been invited the teachers of a junior high school pupil with a problem?

   A. Learning more about the student
   B. Mobilizing resources of the teachers toward aiding the student
   C. Orienting the teachers to the dynamics of overt pupil behavior
   D. Informing teachers of the relation between poor teaching and problem behavior

23. If the P.E. of an I.Q. is 5 points, what proportion of children may be expected to test 5 or more points higher on a retest after correction for practice effect?

   A. 5%   B. 25%   C. 50%   D. 68%

24. If an elementary school of 1500 pupils reflected the distribution of intelligence of the general child population, about how many pupils would be found to have I.Q.'s below 80 on the Stanford-Binet?

   A. 50   B. 100   C. 250   D. 500

25. A tachistoscope is useful in

   A. measuring eye movements   B. testing eye coordination
   C. speeding up word recognition D. determining eye dominance

26. The schizophrenic patient is said to exhibit loss of affect. This amounts to

   A. decreased attention to one's personal feeling tone
   B. lack of emotional reaction toward abstract ideas
   C. increased affectivity to ideas and decreased affectivity concerning persons and events
   D. increased affectiveness in environment but less to abstractions

27. Ability to establish a conditioned response in the eyelid has been found to be a point of differentiation between

   A. idiopathic epilepsy and hysterical seizures
   B. malingering and traumatic neurosis
   C. senile dementia and cerebral arteriosclerosis
   D. hysterical and organic blindness

28. The MAIN distinction between normal grief and reactive neurosis is in the

   A. feelings of inadequacy and unreality
   B. lack of basis in real occurrence
   C. duration and intensity of the emotional display
   D. intellectual retardation

29. Kretschmer's dysplastic type applies to those with

   A. compact, round, fleshy habitus
   B. strong, solid, muscular build
   C. slender bodies, long bones, little muscular strength
   D. conspicuous disharmony due to abnormal functioning of the endocrine glands

30. Which of the following is NOT characteristic of anxiety neurosis?

   A. Increase of irritable tension
   B. Vague somatic complaints
   C. Hypersensitivity to external stimuli
   D. Temporary muscular paralysis of the limbs

31. Involutional melancholia is usually characterized by a

   A. marked motor agitation
   B. motor depression
   C. flight of ideas
   D. loss of affect

32. From our knowledge about hallucinatory phenomena, it can be stated reliably that

   A. hallucinations occur in association with a dream-like state
   B. hallucinations and imagery are similar processes differing only in intensity
   C. mescal-induced hallucinations are not similar to schizophrenic hallucinations
   D. organized hallucinations can be produced by direct stimulation of the brain surface

33. Which of the following is NOT a form of epilepsy?

   A. Grand mal
   B. Pyknolepsy
   C. Jacksonian
   D. Parkinsonian

34. A poor prognostic indication in schizophrenia is

   A. cycloid prepsychotic personality
   B. early onset
   C. good response to sodium amytal
   D. acute onset

35. A consistently maladjusted style of life distinguished by infantilism, egocentricity and a strong tendency to dissociation is typical of

    A. cycloid personality
    B. hysterical personality
    C. epileptoid personality
    D. extroversion

36. The use of the term "parergasia" to denote schizophrenia was advocated by

    A. Bleuler   B. Freud   C. Meyer   D. Kraepelin

37. A child who is just ten years old, has an I.Q. of 80, and has reading ability of grade 3.0, should be considered

    A. a retarded reader, but not a reading disability case
    B. a case of reading disability, but not a retarded reader
    C. both a retarded reader and a case of reading disability
    D. neither a retarded reader nor a case of reading disability

38. In the teaching of reading, silent reading should be introduced

    A. from the beginning of book reading
    B. after good oral reading has been established
    C. after the pupils are able to read primers
    D. after the children can read first readers

39. A set of picture-word cards useful in the teaching of reading has been devised by

    A. Betts   B. Dolch   C. Durrell   D. Herbart

40. In selecting reading material for a retarded reader, with regard to difficulty, it is BEST to

    A. begin with material which is at or below the child's reading level
    B. retrace reading instruction by beginning with first grade material in all cases
    C. use material at the child's present grade but give him a great deal of help with it
    D. use material which is half-way between his reading grade and his present grade-placement

41. A useful inventory of phonetic elements is included in the diagnostic battery of

    A. Monroe   B. Gates   C. Traxler   D. Durrell

42. Modern teaching of the mentally retarded stresses

    A. greater reliance upon memorization and a corresponding de-emphasis upon understanding
    B. closer correlation with life activities, including occupations
    C. reeducation through emotional release and creative activities
    D. recognition that these children need the identical curriculum as the normal but require more time to master it

43. Percentile norms are advantageous because they are

   A. applicable to high school students, for whom age and grade norms have relatively little meaning
   B. more readily calculated and understood than age and grade norms
   C. so derived as to permit direct comparison of mental test results based on different norm groups
   D. more reliable than scores based on medians of age or grade groups

44. The use of the Merrill-Terman abbreviated form of their 1937 Revision of the Stanford-Binet Scale, as compared with the full scale, affects testing time and reliability in accordance with which of the following statements?

   A. It reduces testing time by more than half but increases the percentage of cases showing deviations of more than 5 I.Q. points by more than a third.
   B. It reduces testing time by about a third but increases the percentage of cases showing deviations of more than 5 I.Q. points by more than a third.
   C. It reduces testing time by more than half and increases the percentage of cases showing deviations of more than 5 I.Q. points by a third or less.
   D. It reduces testing time by about a third and increases the percentage of cases showing deviations of more than 5 I.Q. points by a third or less.

45. As compared with the 1937 Stanford-Binet Scale, the Wechsler Intelligence Scale for Children

   A. results in greater variability in I.Q.
   B. yields much lower I.Q.'s for gifted children
   C. results in higher I.Q.'s on the average
   D. yields lower I.Q.'s for retarded children

46. The psychological theory which has proved MOST helpful in dealing with the problems of the brain-injured is

   A. psychoanalysis
   B. Gestalt psychology
   C. behaviorism
   D. functional psychology

47. The Goodenough Draw-a-Man Test, as originally employed, has proved less revealing than the Machover Human Figure Test principally because the Goodenough

   A. dealt with content to the exclusion of formal aspects of the drawing
   B. required that the figure be copied
   C. resulted in a score that was uncorrelated with intelligence
   D. was not interpreted in dynamic terms

48. Assuming constancy of the I.Q., if a child has an M.A. of 8-0 at 10-0 years, what would his M.A. be at 12-6 years?

   A. 8-6   B. 10-0   C. 10-6   D. 11-0

49. McNemar has shown that the standard error of an I.Q. on the Revised Stanford-Binet

    A. varies directly with the size of the obtained I.Q.
    B. varies indirectly with the size of the obtained I.Q.
    C. is independent of the size of the obtained I.Q.
    D. follows a sine curve relationship with the size of the obtained I.Q.

50. Remedial measures regarding such nervous habits as thumb-sucking or excessive restlessness are most effective when they

    A. are directed toward the alleviation of the underlying source of the habit
    B. give the child a meaningful understanding of the disadvantages of continuing the habit
    C. apply the principle of reward and punishment directly to situations in which the habit manifests itself:
    D. prevent any further behavioral manifestations of the habit until the child outgrows the need responsible for it.

KEY (CORRECT ANSWERS)

1. D	11. A	21. D	31. A	41. B
2. C	12. A	22. D	32. D	42. B
3. D	13. A	23. B	33. D	43. A
4. C	14. A	24. B	34. B	44. D
5. C	15. B	25. C	35. B	45. B
6. C	16. D	26. C	36. C	46. B
7. A	17. C	27. D	37. C	47. D
8. C	18. C	28. C	38. A	48. B
9. A	19. A	29. D	39. B	49. A
10. B	20. B	30. D	40. A	50. A

EXAMINATION SECTION
TEST 1

DIRECTIONS: Each question or incomplete statement is followed by several suggested answers or completions. Select the one that BEST answers the question or completes the statement. *PRINT THE LETTER OF THE CORRECT ANSWER IN THE SPACE AT THE RIGHT.*

1. The reliabilities of the individual subtests of the Wechsler Intelligence Scale for Children are
    A. lower at age 7 1/2 than at age 10 1/2
    B. lower at age 10 1/2 than at age 7 1/2
    C. approximately equal to the reliability of the verbal scale
    D. approximately equal to the reliability of the performance scale

2. If the Standard Error of Estimate of a test is 6, an obtained score will probably not vary on retest more than 6 points
    A. 32% of the time
    B. 22% of the time
    C. 68% of the time
    D. 88% of the time

3. An example of negative correlation is the relationship between
    A. reliability and standard error of measurement
    B. variability and standard deviation
    C. IQ and percentile rank
    D. validity and predictability

4. Most empirical studies indicate a correlation of about .75 between the Stanford-Binet and the Wechsler Intelligence Scale for Children. This indicates that
    A. the WISC is less reliable than the Stanford-Binet
    B. only 75% of the WISC I.Q.'s will agree with the Stanford-Binet I.Q.'s
    C. the confidence limits of the WISC I.Q.'s are computed with 25% error
    D. approximately 50% of the variability between the two tests is statistically independent

5. The reliability coefficients of most standardized intelligence tests when compared with the validity coefficients of the same test are generally
    A. significantly higher
    B. significantly lower
    C. approximately equal
    D. either higher or lower depending on the test

6. Among the following, the *HIGHEST* correlation between school marks and IQ's for groups of individuals will most probably be found in
    A. elementary school
    B. high school
    C. college
    D. graduate school

7. A recent research study conducted in a small town school reported a correlation of .85 between 5th grade IQ's and scholastic averages. An objective conclusion is:

A. For this class, level of achievement is determined largely by level of intelligence.
B. For this class, no inferences can be made regarding the effect of intelligence upon level of achievement.
C. Basic errors in statistical computation were probably made.
D. The design of the study was probably inappropriate.

8. Mr. Jones, the principal of a public school, discovers that the children in the fifth grade fall below the national norms for their grade in arithmetic. The psychologist should suggest that

    A. he promptly organize special remedial help in class so that they may reach the norm for their grades
    B. he explain to the teachers that they must motivate the children more constructively so as to improve their work
    C. he promptly organize a program of individual remedial help
    D. none of the above

9. Mrs. Johnson, the principal of the school, asks Mr. Kramer, the psychologist, to inform one of the teachers that she is relieving her of her assignment as guidance counselor. Of the following, the MOST appropriate action the psychologist can take is to

    A. suggest to the principal that she handle this matter herself
    B. point out to the principal that for the psychologist to do so would impair his relationship with the teacher
    C. write a note to the teacher informing her of the action that was taken
    D. discuss the decision with the teacher

10. Mr. Wilson is one of the most popular teachers in the school. He is friendly and soft-spoken. In school he helps children solve their grievances by putting on boxing gloves. In his leisure time he watches wrestling and boxing matches. His favorite programs are murder mysteries and westerns. This description would lead us to the conclusion that Mr. Wilson is MOST probably

    A. basically a passive person
    B. sublimating some of his aggressive drives
    C. experiencing constant frustration
    D. needs psychotherapy

11. Mr. Anderson, a teacher in the school, stops the psychologist who is passing through the hall and points to a boy standing near him. He describes in angry tones how the child struck a girl in the class. He asks him to see the boy to "straighten him out." Of the following the MOST appropriate action for the psychologist to take is to

    A. schedule an early date for psychological testing
    B. discuss with the teacher possible causes of the child's behavior
    C. suggest to the teacher methods of attaining effective discipline in class
    D. point out the effect of the lack of the teacher's objectivity on the child's adjustment

12. If a two-year-old child exhibited temper tantrums, the MOST probable explanation of this behavior would be that he is

    A. reacting to the birth of a sibling
    B. reacting in a fashion appropriate to his stage of development

C. overindulged by his parents, but inconsistently disciplined
D. reacting to a disturbed family situation

13. Robert, age 8, lives with his mother who is separated from her husband. According to the health card no action was taken by the parent in obtaining the recommended glasses and urgent dental work for Robert. Robert frequently comes to school without breakfast and both his face and clothing are dirty. Because he stays out late at night, he falls asleep in class. Of the following, the BEST referral resource to use would be the

     A. Family Service Society
     B. Society for Prevention of Cruelty to Children
     C. Juvenile Aid Bureau
     D. Children's Aid Society

14. The "Directory of Social Agencies of the City of New York" is a publication which is prepared by the

     A. Welfare Council
     B. Department of Welfare
     C. Department of Mental Hygiene
     D. New School for Social Research

15. Malcolm, age 4, gave no human movement responses on the Rorschach. For Malcolm, this is indicative of

     A. sub-normal intelligence   B. emotional constriction
     C. inadequate ego development   D. none of the above

16. Epilepsy is mainly associated with

     A. brain injury   B. migraine
     C. dysrythmia   D. aggressivity

17. A disturbance of language perception and expression is called

     A. aphasia   B. amnesia   C. amentia   D. alexia

18. Alcoholism is MOST commonly connected with

     A. dysrythmia   B. neurosis
     C. psychopathy   D. overt homosexuality

19. The polygraph is MOST useful for diagnosing

     A. epilepsy   B. aggressivity
     C. deception   D. brain damage

20. The electroencephalogram is MOST useful for diagnosing

     A. brain tumor   B. epilepsy
     C. brain injury   D. mental deficiency

21. Shock therapy is MOST likely to be recommended for

     A. paranoid schizophrenics   B. depressed psychotics
     C. severe psychoneurotics   D. psychopaths

22. Prefrontal lobotomy was MOST likely to be recommended for

    A. aggressive psychotics
    B. apathetic psychotics
    C. paranoid psychotics
    D. psychopaths

23. Most authorities believe that mental deficiency is

    A. never hereditary
    B. always hereditary
    C. sometimes hereditary
    D. rarely hereditary

24. Recent experiments utilizing glutamic acid in an attempt to raise the intellectual level of retarded children have resulted in

    A. inconclusive findings
    B. a marked temporary rise in intellectual level
    C. a marked permanent rise in intellectual level
    D. a slight temporary decline in intellectual level

25. An individual's Rorschach protocol may be MOST profitably interpreted in the light of

    A. his behavior while being tested
    B. his case history
    C. his other test results
    D. his presenting problems

26. The Kuder Preference Record tests

    A. attitudes
    B. interests
    C. aptitudes
    D. achievement

27. Personality inventories are LEAST likely to be useful for testing

    A. job applicants
    B. college applicants
    C. military personnel
    D. neuropsychiatric patients

28. In the construction of tests, it is EASIEST to assure oneself of the test's

    A. validity
    B. reliability
    C. objectivity
    D. interpretability

29. If a child's score on a group intelligence test is less than 1 PE (probable error) from the mean score, this score

    A. is not reliable since it is low
    B. is improbable or fallacious
    C. cannot be converted into a percentile score
    D. lies within the middle 50% of the group

30. A report states that a child received a percentile rank of 11. This means that the child was able to

    A. get 11% of the answers correct
    B. get 89% of the answers correct
    C. surpass 11% of the population with which he was compared
    D. surpass 89% of the population with which he was compared

31. In general, correlations between different verbal group intelligence test IQ's of pupils in a given grade may be expected to fall within the range of

    A. .90 - 1.00   B. .70 - .90
    C. .40 - .70   D. .20 - .40

31.____

32. Of the following aspects of intelligence, the one which is measured most *INADE-QUATELY* by present group intelligence tests is

    A. creative imagination
    B. insight into logical relationships
    C. verbal comprehension
    D. mathematical reasoning

32.____

33. The chief *DISADVANTAGE of* teacher-prepared tests is that they

    A. are not sufficiently objective
    B. are too difficult for the average teacher to prepare
    C. lack adequate standardization for grouping purposes within the class
    D. fail to provide a basis for comparison with children in other schools and classes

33.____

34. If it were desirable to convert a pupil's intelligence, reading and arithmetic test scores for the purpose of direct comparison, we would need to know for each test the

    A. percentile rank   B. standard deviation
    C. standard error   D. interquartile range

34.____

35. Lionel obtains a grade score of 2.7 on a valid standardized arithmetic test which you administer. His IQ based on the Binet is 72. In order to approximate whether he is working at capacity in arithmetic you must also know

    A. the range of scores for the class
    B. his chronological age
    C. the mean scores for the class
    D. the reliability of the test

35.____

36. If an unselected group of children Is examined with the Binet at ages 3,8 and 13, then the correlations between the IQ's obtained may be expected to be

    A. highest between ages 8 and 13
    B. highest between ages 3 and 8
    C. highest between ages 3 and 13
    D. closely equivalent for all of the above ages

36.____

37. According to Strauss, the teacher of a brain Injured child should provide

    A. the child with many opportunities for practicing fine motor coordination
    B. a variety of brightly colored illustrations to motivate the child's reading
    C. for frequent isolation of the child from other pupils in the classroom and for special activity
    D. longer than usual work periods before she suggests a change of task to the child

37.____

38. To measure a subject's ability for abstract thinking, the BEST of the following four tests is the

   A. Wechsler-Bellevue
   B. Rorschach
   C. Babcock
   D. Goldstein-Scheerer

39. The major WEAKNESS of projective tests is that

   A. they are too intuitive
   B. they fail to produce consistent findings among different psychologists
   C. their interpretation involves too much projection of the examiner
   D. their validity has not been adequately established

40. Research on child development and adjustment has been MOST severely challenged by the problem of

   A. selecting appropriate statistical methods
   B. predicting future behavior
   C. confirming studies
   D. deriving broad conclusions

41. If a child is mentally retarded, his academic potential can be explained MOST readily to his parent in terms of the status of other children

   A. in his class
   B. of similar CA
   C. of similar MA
   D. of similar IQ

42. It is MOST probable that a school-age child characterized, on the basis of psychological tests, as a mental defective might, in fact, be

   A. epileptic
   B. deaf
   C. mute
   D. schizophrenic

43. The classroom behavior MOST characteristic of the brain injured child includes

   A. distractibility, hyperactivity and lack of inhibition
   B. listlessness, withdrawal and compulsiveness
   C. aggressiveness, fearfulness and egocentrism
   D. perseveration, fatigue and apathy

44. An indispensable condition for effective remedial instruction in reading is

   A. appropriate teaching material
   B. selection of correct teaching methods
   C. frequent regular contacts with the child
   D. proper motivation of the child

45. In oral reading, mixed lateral dominance is MOST often associated with

   A. omissions
   B. substitutions
   C. repetitions
   D. reversals

46. A child's MOST rapid rate of mental growth generally occurs

   A. during the first few months of life
   B. between the ages of 3 - 6
   C. between the ages of 6-12
   D. during early adolescence

47. A psychopath may be distinguished by the fact that he commits antisocial acts   47.____

    A. consistently
    B. without customary reaction to guilt
    C. without awareness of what he is doing
    D. violently

48. Of the following techniques, the one which is considered to be characteristic of non-   48.____
    directive or client-centered therapy is

    A. encouraging transference
    B. reflection of feeling
    C. free association
    D. permissive questioning

49. Psychoanalytic writers consider the MOST important aspect of an analyst's training to be   49.____

    A. his training in psychoanalytic concepts
    B. his training in medicine
    C. his training in analysis
    D. his general psychological training

50. In the transference situation, it is MOST probable that there will be   50.____

    A. positive feeling between analyst and patient
    B. negative feeling between analyst and patient
    C. neutral feeling between analyst and patient
    D. positive and negative feelings between analyst and patient

KEYS (CORRECT ANSWER)

1. A	11. B	21. B	31. B	41. C
2. A	12. B	22. A	32. A	42. D
3. A	13. B	23. C	33. D	43. A
4. D	14. A	24. A	34. B	44. D
5. A	15. D	25. B	35. B	45. D
6. A	16. C	26. B	36. A	46. A
7. B	17. A	27. D	37. C	47. B
8. D	18. B	28. C	38. D	48. B
9. B	19. C	29. D	39. D	49. C
10. B	20. B	30. C	40. B	50. D

TEST 2

DIRECTIONS: Each question or Incomplete statement is followed by several suggested answers or completions. Select the one that BEST answers the question or completes the statement. *PRINT THE LETTER OF THE CORRECT ANSWER IN THE SPACE AT THE RIGHT.*

1. As applied to glandular reactions the prefix "hyper" signifies functioning that is

    A. more than normal
    B. less than normal
    C. qualitatively different but same in amount
    D. atrophied but otherwise normal

    1.____

2. Audrey is a high school girl who has a tendency to stutter. Of the following suggestions as to what her English teacher might do to help Audrey, the one that is *BEST* is to

    A. handle the classroom situation so as to encourage Audrey to relax
    B. call on Audrey suddenly to avoid anticipatory nervousness
    C. urge Audrey to concentrate carefully on each sound as she speaks
    D. have Audrey change her handedness through a series of easily graded exercises

    2.____

3. Sam, a 4th grade pupil who has to wear glasses when he reads, has left his glasses at home, which is two or three blocks from school. Sam offers to go home for them, stating that he forgot them because he was in a hurry to get to school on time. The teacher should

    A. send Sam home for them
    B. send a trusted child to Sam's home for the glasses
    C. have Sam do the regular work without his glasses as a natural punishment for forgetting his glasses
    D. permit Sam to avoid close reading during the morning so as not to strain his eyes

    3.____

4. A teacher states that one of her pupils brings such curious objects to school as a snake's rattlers, an old earphone and a broken carved nutcracker. The teacher should be advised to

    A. ignore the pupil unless other pupils begin to imitate him
    B. give him a monitor's job on condition he promise not to bring odd objects to school
    C. write his parents a politely worded note describing his behavior
    D. utilize these objects in class discussions

    4.____

5. Each day Miss Smith gives a homework assignment which consists of having the pupils write four spelling words ten times each. Miss Smith should be advised to

    A. discontinue the practice since children below the 5th grade should have no written homework assignments
    B. give the assignment only to those who fail to earn about 90% on a daily spelling test
    C. discontinue the practice since repetition in itself does not assure correct spelling
    D. continue the practice not so much to teach spelling as to encourage independent study habits

    5.____

6. A core curriculum is one that is organized about

    A. a large area of living, such as the family
    B. a significant aspect of development, such as language
    C. correlated activities in the fundamental tool subjects
    D. a graded presentation of the minimum essentials of the basic school subjects

7. The two arithmetical processes with which children ordinarily have the greatest *DIFFI-CULTY* are

    A. addition and subtraction
    B. subtraction and division
    C. division and multiplication
    D. multiplication and subtraction

8. In teaching that 12 inches equal 1 foot, 3 feet a yard, and 36 inches a yard, a teacher is *MOST* justified in

    A. providing experiences for discovering these facts before helping the children to relate one fact to another
    B. having the children learn the three facts at one time in order to have them see the relationship of one fact to another
    C. not aiming at complete mastery of these facts since they are readily available, when needed, in reference books accessible to children and adults
    D. having the children first memorize the facts and then giving them problems to solve in which the facts are applied

9. The present tendency in the occupational education of mentally retarded boys is to stress

    A. service trades
    B. woodwork and carpentry
    C. electrical trades
    D. agricultural occupations

10. In psychoanalytic terminology, the adoption of symptoms or organic disorders is known as

    A. transference
    B. conversion
    C. symbolization
    D. fixation

11. Arthur, Ben, Carl and Dan all have I.Q.'s of 70 as measured by the Revised Stanford-Binet Scale. Arthur and Ben are 9 years old; Carl and Dan are 12. Arthur and Carl are birth-injured children; Ben and Dan are cases of familial mental retardation. Assuming each child to be representative of his group, in which child is variability among mental functions likely to be greatest?

    A. Arthur   B. Ben   C. Carl   D. Dan

12. Athetoid reactions are characterized by

    A. rapid, jerky movements
    B. unconsciousness
    C. absence of movement
    D. tentacle-like movements

13. The sequelae of encephalitis

    A. are now preventable in virtually every case of the disease
    B. may become evident long after an acute attack of the disease
    C. respond readily to treatment when detected
    D. are physical and emotional but rarely mental

14. As a school system changes over to a 100% promotion plan, the need for special classes for mentally retarded pupils may be expected to

    A. become more evident as the range of scholastic ability within a single grade becomes greater
    B. apply to pupils entering the kindergarten *as* much as to pupils in the higher grades
    C. virtually disappear because of the elimination of school retardation and failure
    D. increase because of the need to place a larger proportion of intellectually normal but scholastically over-age pupils in special classes

15. The mental mechanism most strongly EMPHASIZED in psychoanalytic formulations of schizophrenia is

    A. repression   B. conversion
    C. projection   D. regression

16. Paranoia differs from the paranoid type of schizophrenia in

    A. the occurrence of delusions in one and not the other
    B. the fact that the paranoid patient does not act on the basis of his delusions
    C. the amount of "psychopathic tainting" in the family history
    D. that the delusions are more systematized

17. According to the Freudian psychoanalysts, the personality changes in general paresis are due to

    A. oedipus complex   B. infantile sex urges
    C. sublimations   D. changes in narcissism

18. A patient who touched his chin when asked to touch his nose would be MOST likely to be suffering from

    A. motor apraxia   B. motor ataxia
    C. sensory apraxia   D. agnosia

19. Shock treatment for schizophrenia, especially by the use of metrazol, was introduced at first because of the theory that

    A. shock arouses special physiological defense mechanisms by way of the "alarm reaction"
    B. shock stimulates the autonomic nervous system and thus facilitates homeostasis
    C. convulsions protect epileptics against developing schizophrenic symptoms
    D. shock as a form of punishment gratifies the patient's masochistic tendencies

20. From his survey of experimental evidence on the effect of infant care on later personality, Orlansky was led to the conclusion that such factors as breast-feeding and toilet-training

    A. are of no significance for later personality
    B. are significant determiners of personality

C. are relevant to personality only insofar as they indicate the mother's attitude, which is the effective factor
D. may help determine personality but constitutional and post-infantile factors should receive major emphasis

21. A part of the nervous system NOT known to have any connection with emotional behavior is referred to as the

    A. parasympathetic nervous system
    B. basal ganglia
    C. frontal lobes of cerebral cortex
    D. temporal lobes of cerebral cortex

22. A phobia is

    A. less specific than anxiety
    B. more specific than anxiety
    C. synonymous with an anxiety
    D. less acute than anxiety

23. The division of the autonomic nervous system that coordinates bodily changes in fear and anger is

    A. sacral
    B. sympathetic
    C. emergency
    D. cranial

24. In estimating intelligence from the Rorschach Test, which one of the following scoring criteria is NOT utilized?

    A. Percent of whole responses
    B. Number of responses that are more determined by color than by form
    C. Number and quality of human movement responses
    D. Number and quality of original responses

25. Wechsler's intelligence test for children differs from his adult scales in that the children's test includes

    A. form board tests
    B. mazes
    C. finger dexterity tests
    D. memory tests

26. Among the qualities considered desirable in a measurement technique are that it have (1) truly equal units and (2) a zero point that signifies "just no amount" of the trait to be measured. The Terman-Merrill Revision of the Stanford-Binet has

    A. both (1) and (2)
    B. (1) but not (2)
    C. (2) but not (1)
    D. neither (1) nor (2)

27. The effect of familiarity in the case of inter-racial attitudes is

    A. dependent upon the nature of the contact
    B. a tendency to breed contempt
    C. greater understanding and acceptance
    D. of little importance one way or the other

28. If a student wanted to find a critical review of the Compass Diagnostic Tests in Arithmetic, the place to look would be

   A. Whipple-Manual of Mental and Physical Tests
   B. The Publisher's Catalogue
   C. Review of Educational Research
   D. Buros-Mental Measurements Yearbook

28._____

29. For guidance work with senior high school students, one would find it MOST generally convenient to work with

   A. age norms
   B. grade norms
   C. percentile norms
   D. quotient norms

29._____

30. For which of the following tests would one be MOST likely to use age norms?

   A. A test of achievement in chemistry
   B. A questionnaire on personal adjustment
   C. An aptitude test for selecting airplane pilots
   D. A spelling test

30._____

31. A student fell at the 60th percentile on a 200-item final examination in biology given to his class of 80 pupils at school. This means that he

   A. was beaten by 48 pupils in the class
   B. was better than 48 pupils in the class
   C. got 120 items right
   D. was more than one standard deviation from the mean

31._____

32. The Navy reports aptitude test results in terms of standard scores with a mean of 50 and a standard deviation of 10. A recruit with a mechanical comprehension score of 65 is a candidate for machinist training. On the basis of this score he would be judged

   A. a very superior candidate
   B. likely to prove about average
   C. a borderline case
   D. a poor risk

32._____

33. A third grade class was given a standardized reading test at the end of the year. The median score, expressed in grade norms, was 4.1. How should the principal evaluate these results?

   A. The group was doing better than should be expected.
   B. Too much emphasis was being given to reading, at the expense of broader educational objectives.
   C. The teacher was an effective teacher of reading.
   D. The information as given is not sufficient to permit an evaluation.

33._____

34. Which of the following procedures would you expect to increase the reliability of a test?

   A. Increasing the length of the test
   B. Increasing the number of people tested
   C. Increasing the number of types of items on the test
   D. Increasing the homogeneity of the group tested

34._____

35. Which of the following procedures is MOST likely to give one a distorted impression of the reliability of a test?   35._____

   A. Combining data from several different communities
   B. Basing the reliability upon test-retest procedures
   C. Reporting reliabilities for boys and girls separately
   D. Computing the reliability for a group including several grades

36. Which of the following statements could NOT possibly be true for an aptitude or an achievement test?   36._____

   A. Though it has little face validity, it shows substantial statistical validity.
   B. Though it is judged to have high content validity, it has very low reliability.
   C. Though it has zero reliability, it has substantial statistical validity.
   D. Though it has zero statistical validity, its reliability is quite high.

37. You have given a multiple-choice examination made up of 4 choice items (like this one), and have decided to correct the results for guessing. Which formula should you use?   37._____

   A. Rights - wrongs
   B. Rights - 1/2 wrongs
   C. Rights - 1/3 wrongs
   D. Rights - 1/4 wrongs

38. Aptitude tests have been developed to select persons for training in such fields as law, medicine, engineering, and the like. Each test for any one of these different jobs   38._____

   A. includes much the same material as is found in tests of general intelligence
   B. is related to success in only one particular type of training
   C. is quite different from tests for the other jobs
   D. is almost uncorrelated with I.Q.

39. Which of the following widely used group tests of intelligence makes the MOST serious attempt to provide diagnostic sub-scores?   39._____

   A. Otis Quick Scoring
   B. Henmon-Nelson
   C. California Mental Maturity
   D. Kuhlmann-Anderson

40. The "Guess Who" technique used in elementary school is a form of   40._____

   A. self-report inventory
   B. projective technique
   C. sociometric technique
   D. problem-solving test

41. Which of the following methods of personality evaluation would depend MOST crucially upon the self-awareness of the person being measured?   41._____

   A. A sociometric test
   B. An adjustment inventory
   C. A rating schedule
   D. A projective test

42. What general difficulty has been found with performance tests of character, such as those of Hartshorn and May?   42._____

   A. The reliability of the tests is extremely low.
   B. The performance measured seems to be very specific to a single narrow type of situation.

C. The tests are very subjective, and call for a great deal of judgment in scoring.
D. They are too much affected by school training.

43. Negativism is MOST typical of children at the age of

   A. one year
   B. three years
   C. six years
   D. nine years

44. Children's groups about the age of two typically show

   A. much cooperation
   B. sex segregation
   C. parallel activity
   D. none of these

45. In Gesell and Thompson's study of the influence of training upon stair climbing in a pair of twins, the control twin showed

   A. as rapid development as the trained twin
   B. a permanent handicap from the loss of training
   C. the ability to catch up with the trained twin with much less training
   D. very little ability to profit from later training

46. In the Wickman study, which of the following classroom behaviors did mental specialists consider MOST serious?

   A. Continuous daydreaming
   B. Defiance of authority
   C. Disorder
   D. Obscene language

47. Studies of growth in relation to the arithmetic curriculum suggest that in the past we tended to teach arithmetic processes

   A. with too much emphasis upon problem-solving
   B. before the child was sufficiently mature to master them efficiently
   C. after the child had lost interest in the fundamental concept of number
   D. too slowly to keep the interest of the average child

48. Most individual growth curves are characterized by

   A. periods of sudden growth alternating with periods of no change
   B. a somewhat irregular, but nevertheless continuous and progressive growth
   C. a smooth, uniform curve of development
   D. none of these

49. If a biology test included the following sub-tests, which one would you expect to show the LEAST loss after a time interval of discontinued learning?

   A. Identification of different organisms
   B. Knowledge of biological facts
   C. Ability to interpret biological experiments
   D. Matching names and experiments

50. In which of the following functions does development depend MOST completely upon maturation?

   A. Roller skating
   B. Swimming
   C. Singing
   D. Walking

KEY (CORRECT ANSWER)

1. A	11. C	21. B	31. B	41. B
2. A	12. D	22. B	32. A	42. B
3. D	13. B	23. D	33. D	43. B
4. D	14. A	24. B	34. A	44. C
5. C	15. D	25. B	35. D	45. C
6. A	16. D	26. D	36. C	46. A
7. C	17. D	27. A	37. C	47. B
8. A	18. A	28. D	38. A	48. B
9. A	19. C	29. C	39. C	49. C
10. B	20. D	30. D	40. C	50. D

TEST 3

DIRECTIONS: Each question or Incomplete statement is followed by several suggested answers or completions. Select the one that BEST answers the question or completes the statement. *PRINT THE LETTER OF THE CORRECT ANSWER IN THE SPACE AT THE RIGHT.*

1. In the first months of an infant's life, the baby's reflex responses are

    A. almost the only reactions the baby shows
    B. virtually absent from behavior
    C. more accurate than later in life
    D. less conspicuous than generalized mass reactions

    1.____

2. Play and reading interests of boys and girls will be found to be most DIFFERENT at the age of

    A. three years
    B. six years
    C. twelve years
    D. eighteen years

    2.____

3. The unsociability often reported for very bright children is MOST likely to be due to

    A. their biological makeup
    B. their complete absorption in intellectual pursuits
    C. their lack of personal attractiveness
    D. the absence of suitable companions

    3.____

4. If we measure a number of individuals upon a variety of complex mental functions, we will find that the different functions show

    A. a negative relationship
    B. no relationship
    C. a fairly high degree of positive relationship
    D. practically a perfect positive relationship

    4.____

5. As children in groups with very limited environments, such as canal-boat dwellers, "hollow-folk," etc., grow older, their I.Q. is found to

    A. increase
    B. stay the same
    C. decrease
    D. vary widely and irregularly

    5.____

6. Which of the following BEST characterizes Hildreth's BIBLIOGRAPHY OF TESTS AND RATING SCALES (together with its supplement)?

    A. Full description of each test listed
    B. Critical comments on each test listed
    C. Virtually complete listing of all tests and scales
    D. All of the above

    6.____

7. Forgetting curves are characterized by

    A. a more rapid initial drop followed by slower forgetting
    B. a constant rate of loss

    7.____

C. a slow drop at first, with more rapid loss
D. none of these

8. Formulation of rules, definitions, and verbal generalizations

    A. has virtually no place in the process of learning
    B. should be the final outcome of learning
    C. should accompany and be accompanied by actual experience
    D. should be the first step in any learning

9. Transfer from one subject to another or to life situations will be increased if

    A. techniques and applications are emphasized
    B. the first subject is very difficult
    C. a good deal of drill is given in the first subject
    D. the situations seem quite different

10. Of the following general statements about deterioration in mental patients, which is the most QUESTIONABLE at present?

    A. More recently acquired forms of reaction are lost before those formed earlier in life.
    B. Generalization and abstraction in psychoses is qualitatively the same as that in the young child.
    C. Deterioration in many cases regarded as hopeless appears to be reversible.
    D. The responses of a deteriorated person show generally a definite patterning which tends to mask his defects.

11. Concerning the course of intellectual deterioration in the mental disorders, it is CORRECT to state that

    A. defect in the ability to generalize is more characteristic of schizophrenia than of other psychotic states
    B. concept formation deteriorates more slowly in schizophrenia than in senile psychosis
    C. decreased speed and persistence in mental activity are characteristic of epilepsy
    D. senile patients suffer more impairment in the recall of long past events than in recent memory

12. According to mental test comparisons of cooperative patients in the various disease groups, the group which shows the LEAST intellectual impairment is

    A. paranoid schizophrenia
    B. psychopathic personality
    C. hebephrenic schizophrenia
    D. hysteria

13. Schizophrenic speech is BEST characterized by

    A. loose, approximate use of words and reaction to superficial similarities among ideas and objects
    B. loose, approximate use of words and failure to make use of similarities or analogies

C. unusual amount of stammering and reaction to superficial similarities among ideas and objects
D. unusual amount of stammering and failure to make use of similarities or analogies

14. It is the central, distinguishing feature of the depressive phase of manic-depressive psychosis that

    A. the patient is keenly aware of lacking a motive for existence
    B. the patient attaches his depression to some irrelevant or imaginary cause
    C. the patient is excessively disturbed over some recent trouble
    D. the patient is overactive, restless, and even agitated

15. According to the Doctrine of Formal Discipline, the study of Latin is valuable because

    A. an educated individual should know Latin
    B. the study of a difficult subject strengthens the intellect in general
    C. many English words come from Latin
    D. Latin helps with other college subjects

16. According to studies reported by Edward L. Thorndike, ability to learn

    A. is greatest in early childhood
    B. increases throughout life
    C. reaches a maximum in the thirtees and then drops rapidly
    D. reaches a maximum in the twenties and then drops slowly

17. Problem-solving behavior, according to the views of E.L. Thorndike,

    A. first makes its appearance at adolescence
    B. first makes its appearance at the age of about 10 years and grows rapidly from then to adolescence
    C. is present in rudimentary form in pre-school children and develops gradually throughout the whole school career
    D. is clearly evident in superior children at birth

18. In which of the following abilities do dull and gifted children tend to differ most markedly?

    A. Arithmetical computation
    B. Drawing
    C. Reading comprehension
    D. Spelling

19. Which of the following statements reflects an attitude concerning anecdotal records that would be soundest to take?

    A. Even if not entirely accurate, anecdotal records reveal how his teachers probably perceive a pupil.
    B. Such records are useful only when limited to unbiased reports of overt behavior as recorded by trained specialists.
    C. Despite their limitations, anecdotal records are more valid than any other method of appraising personality.
    D. Anecdotal records are bound to be unreliable because teachers are biased favorably or otherwise according to how well a pupil behaves.

20. Regardless of one's standpoint, it is generally desirable in a series of counseling interviews for the counselor to

    A. structure with the client in advance the topics to be discussed
    B. structure the interviews as one goes along
    C. prevent the client from structuring the interview
    D. avoid structuring the interview on one's own part

21. A high school senior with a good record in mathematics has been referred to the school psychologist because of a drop in his grades. When asked for his opinion as to why his math grades have deteriorated, he complains that his math teacher doesn't explain the work and that when the student does poorly on a test, she says he should be able to do better, but doesn't help him. The school psychologist should

    A. recommend a transfer to another mathematics class
    B. suggest to the teacher that she consider whether the use of concrete materials would not increase student comprehension
    C. discuss the student's complaint with the chairman of the mathematics department
    D. do none of the above

22. Which of the following represents the *LEAST* valuable use to which a school psychologist can put a case conference to which have been invited the teachers of a junior high school pupil with a problem?

    A. Learning more about the student
    B. Mobilizing resources of the teachers toward aiding the student
    C. Orienting the teachers to the dynamics of overt pupil behavior
    D. Informing teachers of the relation between poor teaching and problem behavior

23. If the P.E. of an I.Q. is 5 points, what proportion of children may be expected to test 5 or more points higher on a retest after correction for practice effect?

    A. 5%   B. 25%   C. 50%   D. 68%

24. If an elementary school of 1500 pupils reflected the distribution of intelligence of the general child population, about how many pupils would be found to have I.Q.'s below 80 on the Stanford-Binet?

    A. 50   B. 100   C. 250   D. 500

25. A tachistoscope is useful in

    A. measuring eye movements
    B. testing eye coordination
    C. speeding up word recognition
    D. determining eye dominance

26. The schizophrenic patient is said to exhibit loss of affect. This amounts to

    A. decreased attention to one's personal feeling tone
    B. lack of emotional reaction toward abstract ideas
    C. increased affectivity to ideas and decreased affectivity concerning persons and events
    D. increased affectiveness in environment but less to abstractions

27. Ability to establish a conditioned response in the eyelid has been found to be a point of differentiation between

   A. idiopathic epilepsy and hysterical seizures
   B. malingering and traumatic neurosis
   C. senile dementia and cerebral arteriosclerosis
   D. hysterical and organic blindness

28. The MAIN distinction between normal grief and reactive neurosis is in the

   A. feelings of inadequacy and unreality
   B. lack of basis in real occurrence
   C. duration and intensity of the emotional display
   D. intellectual retardation

29. Kretschmer's dysplastic type applies to those with

   A. compact, round, fleshy habitus
   B. strong, solid, muscular build
   C. slender bodies, long bones, little muscular strength
   D. conspicuous disharmony due to abnormal functioning of the endocrine glands

30. Which of the following is NOT characteristic of anxiety neurosis?

   A. Increase of irritable tension
   B. Vague somatic complaints
   C. Hypersensitivity to external stimuli
   D. Temporary muscular paralysis of the limbs

31. Involutional melancholia is usually characterized by a

   A. marked motor agitation   B. motor depression
   C. flight of ideas   D. loss of affect

32. From our knowledge about hallucinatory phenomena, it can be stated reliably that

   A. hallucinations occur in association with a dream-like state
   B. hallucinations and imagery are similar processes differing only in intensity
   C. mescal-induced hallucinations are not similar to schizophrenic hallucinations
   D. organized hallucinations can be produced by direct stimulation of the brain surface

33. Which of the following is NOT a form of epilepsy?

   A. Grand mal   B. Pyknolepsy
   C. Jacksonian   D. Parkinsonian

34. A poor prognostic indication in schizophrenia is

   A. cycloid prepsychotic personality
   B. early onset
   C. good response to sodium amytal
   D. acute onset

35. A consistently maladjusted style of life distinguished by infantilism, egocentricity and a strong tendency to dissociation is typical of

    A. cycloid personality
    B. hysterical personality
    C. epileptoid personality
    D. extroversion

36. The use of the term "parergasia" to denote schizophrenia was advocated by

    A. Bleuler   B. Freud   C. Meyer   D. Kraepelin

37. A child who is just ten years old, has an I.Q. of 80, and has reading ability of grade 3.0, should be considered

    A. a retarded reader, but not a reading disability case
    B. a case of reading disability, but not a retarded reader
    C. both a retarded reader and a case of reading disability
    D. neither a retarded reader nor a case of reading disability

38. In the teaching of reading, silent reading should be introduced

    A. from the beginning of book reading
    B. after good oral reading has been established
    C. after the pupils are able to read primers
    D. after the children can read first readers

39. A set of picture-word cards useful in the teaching of reading has been devised by

    A. Betts   B. Dolch   C. Durrell   D. Herbart

40. In selecting reading material for a retarded reader, with regard to difficulty, it is BEST to

    A. begin with material which is at or below the child's reading level
    B. retrace reading instruction by beginning with first grade material in all cases
    C. use material at the child's present grade but give him a great deal of help with it
    D. use material which is half-way between his reading grade and his present grade-placement

41. A useful inventory of phonetic elements is included in the diagnostic battery of

    A. Monroe   B. Gates   C. Traxler   D. Durrell

42. Modern teaching of the mentally retarded stresses

    A. greater reliance upon memorization and a corresponding de-emphasis upon understanding
    B. closer correlation with life activities, including occupations
    C. reeducation through emotional release and creative activities
    D. recognition that these children need the identical curriculum as the normal but require more time to master it

43. Percentile norms are advantageous because they are

    A. applicable to high school students, for whom age and grade norms have relatively little meaning
    B. more readily calculated and understood than age and grade norms

C. so derived as to permit direct comparison of mental test results based on different norm groups
D. more reliable than scores based on medians of age or grade groups

44. The use of the Merrill-Terman abbreviated form of their Revision of the Stanford-Binet Scale, as compared with the full scale, affects testing time and reliability in accordance with which of the following statements?

   A. It reduces testing time by more than half but increases the percentage of cases showing deviations of more than 5 I.Q. points by more than a third.
   B. It reduces testing time by about a third but increases the percentage of cases showing deviations of more than 5 I.Q. points by more than a third.
   C. It reduces testing time by more than half and increases the percentage of cases showing deviations of more than 5 I.Q. points by a third or less.
   D. It reduces testing time by about a third and increases the percentage of cases showing deviations of more than 5 I.Q. points by a third or less.

45. As compared with the Stanford-Binet Scale, the Wechsler Intelligence Scale for Children

   A. results in greater variability in I.Q.
   B. yields much lower I.Q.'s for gifted children
   C. results in higher I.Q.'s on the average
   D. yields lower I.Q.'s for retarded children

46. The psychological theory which has proved MOST helpful in dealing with the problems of the brain-injured is

   A. psychoanalysis   B. Gestalt psychology
   C. behaviorism   D. functional psychology

47. The Goodenough Draw-a-Man Test, as originally employed, has proved less revealing than the Machover Human Figure Test principally because the Goodenough

   A. dealt with content to the exclusion of formal aspects of the drawing
   B. required that the figure be copied
   C. resulted in a score that was uncorrelated with intelligence
   D. was not interpreted in dynamic terms

48. Assuming constancy of the I.Q., if a child has an M.A. of 8-0 at 10-0 years, what would his M.A. be at 12-6 years?

   A. 8-6   B. 10-0   C. 10-6   D. 11-0

49. McNemar has shown that the standard error of an I.Q. on the Revised Stanford-Binet

   A. varies directly with the size of the obtained I.Q.
   B. varies indirectly with the size of the obtained I.Q.
   C. is independent of the size of the obtained I.Q.
   D. follows a sine curve relationship with the size of the obtained I.Q.

50. Remedial measures regarding such nervous habits as thumb-sucking or excessive restlessness are most effective when they
    A. are directed toward the alleviation of the underlying source of the habit
    B. give the child a meaningful understanding of the disadvantages of continuing the habit
    C. apply the principle of reward and punishment directly to situations in which the habit manifests itself
    D. prevent any further behavioral manifestations of the habit until the child outgrows the need responsible for it

KEY (CORRECT ANSWER)

1. D	11. A	21. D	31. A	41. B
2. C	12. A	22. D	32. D	42. B
3. D	13. A	23. B	33. D	43. A
4. C	14. A	24. B	34. B	44. D
5. C	15. B	25. C	35. B	45. B
6. C	16. D	26. C	36. C	46. B
7. A	17. C	27. D	37. C	47. D
8. C	18. C	28. C	38. A	48. B
9. A	19. A	29. D	39. B	49. A
10. B	20. B	30. D	40. A	50. A

TEST 4

DIRECTIONS: Each question or Incomplete statement is followed by several suggested answers or completions. Select the one that BEST answers the question or completes the statement. *PRINT THE LETTER OF THE CORRECT ANSWER IN THE SPACE AT THE RIGHT.*

1. Bill's mother has been called to school because Bill's aggressive behavior has got him into disciplinary difficulties with his teacher. In speaking with the mother, the *FIRST* thing the teacher should attempt to do is to

    A. understand and respond to the feelings of the mother in the situation
    B. explain to the parent her responsibility for the child's behavior
    C. point out to the mother specifically which of her attitudes toward the boy needs changing
    D. propose suitable counseling agencies that might be consulted

2. It is often very difficult for the parents of a mentally retarded child to accept their child's retardation. The psychologist who has completed his diagnostic study of a mentally retarded child and is called upon to interpret the findings to the parents can meet the parents' resistant attitude *BEST* by

    A. reassuring the parents that the medical profession has recently embarked on a promising program of research that may discover means of improving the child's condition
    B. acknowledging how the parents must feel and attempting to alleviate such feelings of guilt that may be present by suggesting things the parents can do to help the child
    C. explaining that the examination was thorough and objective, and that reality must be accepted no matter how unpleasant
    D. urging upon the parents the view that high intelligence can be a handicap, and that many retarded children can develop unusually special talents

3. Which one of the following statements best characterizes the meaning of empathy in the counseling situation? The counselor

    A. sympathizes with the client
    B. understands the dynamics of the client's behavior
    C. is genuinely interested in the welfare of the client
    D. can share the client's reactions

4. Studies by Lewin and his associates, in which authoritarian and democratic methods of leadership were compared, suggest that authoritarian leadership in the classroom is *MOST* likely to

    A. be less effective in developing responsibility in the students
    B. be more effective in developing self-discipline in the students
    C. result in a greater amount of aggressiveness of the students to one another
    D. be accompanied by a more apathetic attitude toward their work on the part of students

5. Of the following statements regarding the comparison of the Kuder Preference Record and the Strong Vocational Interest Blank, the *UNTRUE* statement is:

A. The items on the Kuder are equally weighted; those on the Strong are not.
B. Studies show that both of them are moderately related to job satisfaction.
C. The Kuder is more easily scored than the Strong.
D. Studies show that the Kuder is more subject to change during high school days than the Strong.

6. A high school pupil has been very moody and unhappy in school. Upon investigation it is learned that the source of the difficulty lies in parental discord and parental problems at home. The mother requests the name of an agency to which she can go for help with her domestic difficulties. She should be referred to the   6._____

   A. Community Service Society
   B. Social Service Exchange
   C. Bureau of Child Guidance
   D. Domestic Relations Court

Questions 7-10.

Questions 7-10 are based on the following class incident:

The teacher of a Fifth Grade class has left his class at handwork for a few minutes to go to the neighboring supply room for more materials. When he returns, John and Edward, two of the bigger boys, are engaged in a fight.

7. The FIRST thing the teacher should do is to   7._____

   A. shout to John and Edward to stop fighting immediately
   B. ignore the interruption
   C. walk quickly to the combatants and separate them
   D. send one of the larger boys to stop the belligerents

8. In order to prevent a recurrence of such fighting between these two boys, the teacher should   8._____

   A. send for the principal immediately since such behavior is very serious
   B. take their handwork away and deprive them of the privilege of doing handwork for one week
   C. send for their parents
   D. hold a conference with the boys later in the day or after school, listen to their grievances, and try to resolve their differences

9. John claims that Edward started the fight by pushing him. Edward says he bumped into John by accident and John immediately punched him. The teacher knows that John gets into fights more frequently than does Edward. The boys' statements suggest that   9._____

   A. one of the boys must be intentionally lying
   B. it was John's fault and he should be punished
   C. Edward is overly sensitive
   D. each boy may be giving an honest account of the situation as he understands it

10. Even when the teacher has seen the quarrel start and knows that John is the one who began it, John always seems to be sincere when he insists that Edward starts their frequent little fights. This type of distorted thinking is called   10._____

A. projection
B. transference
C. identification
D. regression

Questions 11 - 14.

Questions 11 - 14 are based on the following class incident:
At ten o'clock one morning, one of the boys in Miss Jones' class fell to the floor and began to twitch and writhe all over.

11. Which of the following should *NOT* be done? 11.____

   A. Quickly move or pad any furniture against which the boy may hurt himself
   B. Open the boy's shirt collar
   C. Pour some cold water over the boy's face
   D. Place a pencil between the boy's teeth

12. The kind of "fit" described above is indicative of 12.____

   A. grand mal epilepsy
   B. petit mal epilepsy
   C. Jacksonian epilepsy
   D. Parkinsonian syndrome

13. To have this incident exert the *LEAST* harmful effect upon the other children, Miss Jones should 13.____

   A. have them join another class which is going to the school playground for games
   B. have the two strongest boys carry the boy to the teachers' rest room
   C. tell the children to remain in their seats but to go on with their individual work
   D. have one of the older children lead the class in group singing

14. After the boy regains consciousness, Miss Jones should 14.____

   A. send him home immediately in the company of an older pupil
   B. have him rest for the remainder of the morning
   C. have him resume his classroom activities
   D. give him deep-breathing exercises with the window open
   E.

Questions 15 - 21.

Questions 15 - 21 refer to Helen, a ten year old pupil who has just been admitted into a class for slow learners.

Her former teacher reports that Helen's attendance and punctuality record is good and that her paintings show she is much better than most children of her age. Her reading ability is reported as being relatively good, but she has a strong distaste for arithmetic. Her former teacher indicates further that Helen is weak in the practice of social amenities and seems to have little awareness of the concept of democratic behavior.

15. The teacher's *FIRST* step in planning for Helen's development should be to help her to 15.____

   A. bring her arithmetic level up to her reading age
   B. use her ability in painting to explore her interests and capacities in other areas
   C. try to help Helen succeed in her social relations with other members of the class group

D. develop the appreciational aspect of her education to insure a well-balanced personality

16. Helen's dislike for arithmetic can BEST be replaced with a more positive attitude by

    A. citing cases of adults who, in later life, regretted they had not learned arithmetic
    B. creating situations in which she has to use simple arithmetic
    C. continued drill in basic computations she has not mastered
    D. the use of number tricks and puzzle devices

17. In the light of Helen's ability in painting, the teacher should

    A. introduce the girl to varied art media
    B. launch an art appreciation unit that would benefit the whole class
    C. suggest that Helen study techniques of famous artists to improve her work
    D. discuss with her parents the possibility of a career in art

18. One morning Helen arrives just after the bell has rung and unobtrusively slips into her seat. Wise class management indicates that

    A. the teacher should say nothing about the incident
    B. the girl needs a reminder of the importance of the habit of punctuality
    C. a comment on Helen's sneaking to her seat is in order
    D. Helen be questioned to prevent a recurrence of the tardiness

19. During a recreation period, Helen's teacher notes that Helen is jumping rope with a group of girls from a class for intellectually gifted pupils at the school. The teacher should

    A. ask Helen to play with the girls of her own class
    B. caution Helen not to pay attention to remarks about the fact that she is in a slow class
    C. make no comment at all and allow Helen to continue playing with the group
    D. compliment the girls for their acceptance of Helen in their group

20. Helen fails to follow one of the rules for the proper handling of tools, although her attention has been called to the rule once before. The teacher should

    A. have the girl write the rule a number of times until she can repeat it verbatim
    B. stop the girl's work and remind her never to violate the rule again
    C. warn Helen that the next time she violates the rules she will be barred from arts and crafts work
    D. re-explain and demonstrate the correct use of the tools

21. As applied to Helen, the teacher's acceptance of the principle of "Equal Opportunity for All" would be evidenced by

    A. teaching Helen the minimum essentials of the common school curriculum through the sixth grade
    B. arranging Helen's daily program so that the amount of time available for arts and crafts is the same as that for normal children
    C. advising the parents that the opportunity for a free education for all children to the age of seventeen is a right and obligation that should not be denied
    D. exploring Helen's interests and capacities and providing suitable experience for their development

Questions 22 - 23.

Questions 22 - 23 refer to the appraisal of notations made by a teacher in accordance with the suggestion by her supervisor that she compile anecdotal records of her pupils with a view toward gathering data that might throw a light on their developmental progress and needs.

22. John is always examining other pupils' desks as though he is ready to take anything they leave unguarded. Although I am careful not to give him any opportunity to steal, he needs to be watched lest he become a thief.
As exemplifying what should be included in an anecdotal record, this notation is

   A. commendable because it points to a specific source of John's difficulty
   B. commendable because it is realistic
   C. poor because it is unnecessarily subjective
   D. poor because it depicts an undesirable rather than a positive trait

22.____

23. When called on this morning, Eli gave an excellent description of how a bell works. Before being called on, however, he did not volunteer an answer although no one else seemed able to answer the question.
As exemplifying what should be included in an anecdotal record, this notation is

   A. commendable because it brings to light the need for retesting Eli to determine his true intellectual ability
   B. commendable because it offers a lead to a significant personality characteristic that may require attention
   C. poor because it is unnecessarily long and detailed
   D. poor because Eli should be permitted to volunteer or not, as he pleases

23.____

Questions 24 - 28.

Questions 24 - 28 are based on the following situation:

Jane, 6 years old, has been referred to the Bureau of Child Guidance for testing because she seems obviously backward and unable to function in a regular first grade. The psychologist's findings are: CA 6-4, MA 3-0, IQ 47. Jane has a mild spastic monoplegia, an internal strabismus, a cranial circumference of 20 inches, and a pale, delicate skin, and is subject to intermittent petit mal symptoms. Jane is described as docile, affectionate, and shy. Her speech is indistinct and immature. She has two normal brothers and a normal sister. Her father runs a butcher shop and her mother went through the second year of high school.

24. The test that the Bureau of Child Guidance psychologist probably used was

   A. The Merrill-Palmer Pre-School Scale
   B. The original Binet-Simon Scale
   C. The Revised Stanford-Binet Scale
   D. The Gesell Developmental Schedules

24.____

25. Which of the following symptoms would you expect Jane to show?

   A. severe epileptic convulsions
   B. hysterical outbursts

25.____

C. brief losses of consciousness without falling down
D. periods of great irritability

26. From the information given, it seems MOST probable that the cause of Jane's mental retardation is

   A. a Mendelian recessive characteristic
   B. cerebral birth injury
   C. inherited microcephaly
   D. severe thyroid deficiency

26._____

27. From the description given, one should expect Jane to show

   A. cross-eyes
   B. near sightedness
   C. far-sightedness
   D. astigmatism

27._____

28. In view of her "mild spastic monoplegia" Jane MOST probably has

   A. one limp, nearly useless arm
   B. one stiffened leg
   C. a partial paralysis of one arm and one leg
   D. a partial paralysis of both legs

28._____

Questions 29 - 30.

Questions 29 - 30 are based on the following data: Correlation of Stanford-Binet M.A. with
   Arithmetical computation: .50
   Reading comprehension: .70

29. From these data it is correct to infer that the standard error of prediction from Stanford-Binet M.A. to scores in Arithmetical computation and Reading comprehension, respectively, is likely to be a proportion of the standard error of the respective total distributions, that is

   A. less than 50% in the case of both Arithmetic and Reading
   B. less than 50% in the case of Reading but not Arithmetic
   C. more than 50% in the case of both Arithmetic and Reading
   D. more than 50% in the case of Arithmetic but not Reading

29._____

30. Assuming that standardized tests of Arithmetical computation and Reading comprehension were used, we would expect to find from these data that

   A. mentally accelerated pupils would tend to have a lower average grade equivalent in Arithmetic than in Reading
   B. mentally accelerated pupils would tend to have a higher average grade equivalent in Arithmetic than in Reading
   C. pupils at all mental levels would tend to have a lower average grade equivalent in Arithmetic than in Reading
   D. mentally retarded pupils would tend to have a lower score than mentally accelerated pupils in Reading but not Arithmetic

30._____

Questions 31 - 35.

Questions 31 - 35 are based upon the following case description:

Albert was referred for psychological examination because at the age of 11-6 he is still a total non-reader. His I.Q. is found to be 86. The psychologist notes that in performance tests he does much better with tests involving pictures than in block-design tests, and that in taking the Rorschach he begins on each card by listing the colors on it.

31. On the basis of these two indications, the psychologist should look carefully for further evidence of

    A. neurotic instability
    B. organic brain defect
    C. psychopathic impulsiveness
    D. schizoid trends

32. To check the adequacy of Albert's efficiency in binocular vision, which of the following instruments could be used best ? A

    A. flashmeter
    B. metron-o-scope
    C. telebinocular
    D. visuoscope

33. The psychologist finds that Albert used to be left handed but is now right handed. If the psychologist accepts Orton's theory, he will conclude that

    A. emotional disturbance was created by the way in which Albert was forced to use his right hand
    B. there is a conflict between a natural tendency to move from right to left and an imposed pattern of movement from left to right
    C. there is confusion between memory traces in Albert's left and right cerebral hemispheres
    D. there is no causal relationship between Albert's handedness and his reading disability

34. A series of diagnostic reading tests that could be used profitably by the psychologist examining Albert was devised by

    A. G.L. Buswell
    B. M. Monroe
    C. S.L. Pressey
    D. L.L. Thurstone

35. After further study, the psychologist decides to recommend the use of the Fernald method of teaching non-readers. This method places great emphasis upon

    A. developing visual memory through tachistoscopic presentation of digits, letters and sounds
    B. learning letter sounds and how to blend them
    C. using work books in which words are associated with pictures
    D. tracing words and then writing them from memory

Questions 36 - 40.

Questions 36 - 40 are based on the computational data tabulated below :

FIGURE I

Score	f	x^1	fx^1	$f(x^1)^2$	Cum f
60-66	5	3	15	45	80
53-59	12	2	24	48	75
46-52	26	1	26	26	63
39-45	19	0			37
32-38	10	-1	-10	10	18
25-31	6	-2	-12	24	8
18-24	2	-3	- 6	18	2
N =80			$\Sigma fx^1 =37$	$\Sigma f(x^1)^2 =171$	

36. For the data given in Figure I, the median is closest to the number　　36.____

 A. 39　　B. 40　　C. 46　　D. 52

37. For the data given in Figure I, the correct computation for the arithmetic mean is　　37.____

 A. 42 + 37/80　　B. 42 - 37/80
 C. 42 + (37/80)7　　D. 42 - (80/37)7

38. For the data given in Figure I, the standard deviation is approximately　　38.____

 A. 1.5 units of score　　B. 2 units of score
 C. 5 units of score　　D. 10 units of score

39. For the data given in Figure I, an individual with a score of 32 falls approximately at the　　39.____

 A. 10th percentile　　B. 30th percentile
 C. 50th percentile　　D. 70th percentile

40. An ogive curve can MOST readily be plotted from the information shown in the column in Figure I labelled　　40.____

 A. f　　B. fx^1　　C. $f(x^1)^2$　　D. Cum f

Questions 41 - 43.

Questions 41-43 refer to the following statements from a study by Fiedler of the therapist-patient relationship in three schools of psychotherapy:

1. Expert psychotherapists of any of the three schools create a relationship more closely approximating the Ideal Therapeutic Relationship than relationships created by nonexperts.
2. The therapeutic relationship created by experts of one school resembles more closely that created by experts of other schools than it resembles relationships created by non-experts within the same school.

3. The most important dimension (of those measured) which differentiates experts from nonexperts is related to the therapist's ability to understand, to communicate with, and to maintain rapport with the patient.

41. The statements from Fiedler support the characterization of the expert in psychotherapy as being

    A. effective semantically
    B. an impressive authority figure
    C. a verbalist
    D. thoroughly permissive

41._____

42. In the statements, Fiedler is arguing for

    A. good relationship regardless of school
    B. clear adherence to a school regardless of relationship
    C. good relationship and adherence to a school
    D. less insistence on either kind of relationship or adherence to a school

42._____

43. The central thought embodied in Fiedler's statements is that

    A. the personality of the therapist is more important than his expertness
    B. experts in psychotherapy may differ in certain respects but have certain essentials in common
    C. all three schools of therapy are at fault in neglecting the importance of relationship
    D. client gains in psychotherapy result from internal recuperative processes rather than external efforts

43._____

Questions 44 - 50.

Questions 44-50 are to be answered in the light of the tenets promulgated by Carl Rogers and the other adherents of non-directive counseling.

44. Of the following the most fundamental tenet of non-directive counseling is

    A. that the client has the capacity to bring about changes in his self-concept and behavior
    B. that the counselor should assume a passive role from the beginning and maintain it throughout the sessions
    C. the ideological rejection of psychoanalytic theory and method except as applied to cases of psychosis
    D. that the counselor must refuse to offer advice or information that the client can evolve or discover for himself

44._____

45. Of the following duties of a counselor in a high school the primary one is to

    A. select colleges or jobs appropriate to the abilities and interests of graduating students
    B. handle emotional and adjustive phases of disciplinary problems referred by school administration

45._____

C. use personality inventories to screen out students in need of psychiatric attention
D. aid the students to find solutions to educational and personal guidance problems they bring up

46. In the initial counseling interview, of the following the objective that is most important is to

A. get all the facts pertaining to the problem
B. set forth fully the scope and function of the agency
C. establish a sound working relationship with the client
D. inspire confidence by reassuring the client concerning your ability to solve his problems

47. "Reflection of the client's feelings" refers to the counselor's

A. reiteration of the client's words without modifying his response
B. restatement of the gist of what the client has said without using his words
C. statement of the attitudes evidently embodied in what the client has said
D. interpretation of the dynamics implied in the client's remarks

48. It is good counseling practice to convey interpretation of test results in the case of adolescents

A. as soon as they are available
B. whenever appropriate in the course of counseling sessions
C. whenever the client asks to have the results
D. whenever the client's parent asks for the results

49. A teacher brings a Ninth Grade boy to a school counselor and in the presence of the boy states that "this boy is impossible." Of the following courses of action for the counselor to take, the BEST is to ask

A. the teacher why she finds the boy impossible
B. the boy why he does not control his behavior
C. the teacher how she thought the counselor could be of help
D. the teacher and the boy to wait while the cumulative record is sent for

50. When in conferring with a counselor a student confesses that he has done something he thinks wrong, the counselor should

A. confirm the student's judgment that what he did was wrong
B. urge the student not to do it again
C. seek to prevent guilt feelings by assuring the student that we all make mistakes
D. express neither approval or disapproval

KEY (CORRECT ANSWER)

1. A	11. C	21. D	31. B	41. A
2. B	12. A	22. C	32. C	42. A
3. D	13. C	23. B	33. C	43. B
4. A	14. B	24. C	34. B	44. A
5. D	15. C	25. C	35. D	45. D
6. A	16. B	26. B	36. C	46. C
7. C	17. A	27. A	37. C	47. C
8. D	18. A	28. B	38. D	48. B
9. D	19. C	29. C	39. A	49. C
10. A	20. D	30. A	40. D	50. D

TEST 5

DIRECTIONS: Each question or Incomplete statement is followed by several suggested answers or completions. Select the one that BEST answers the question or completes the statement. *PRINT THE LETTER OF THE CORRECT ANSWER IN THE SPACE AT THE RIGHT.*

1. A Rorschach sign which increases with the mental maturity of the child is   1.____

   A. C B. Do C. DW D. W+

2. The Murray Thematic Apperception Test comprises a series of   2.____

   A. incomplete sentences B. musical themes
   C. pictures D. stories

3. In the administration of the Murray Thematic Apperception Test how much time is the subject given to respond to each item?   3.____

   A. Ten seconds to a card B. One minute to a card
   C. Five minutes to a card D. Unlimited time

4. A mother whose nine-year-old son is a feeding problem at home (he dawdles over his food, has violent food prejudices, and vomits often) visited the school lunch room one day and was amazed to see her youngster eating at the table with his classmates and doing as well as the others. When she discusses this experience with the psychologist to whom the child has been referred for study, the psychologist should try to get her to see that, in all likelihood, her son eats better at school because of   4.____

   A. firm discipline on the part of the teachers
   B. more attractive cooking in the school lunchroom
   C. less emotional tension at meal time
   D. greater need for food intake after mentally fatiguing school work

5. It is generally accepted among those who advocate the most modern methods of parental counseling that, with regard to help in handling children presenting adjustive difficulties, parents   5.____

   A. are inclined to seek direct advice but need to develop insight
   B. seek to develop insight but need to be given direct advice
   C. are inclined to seek direct advice and need to be given direct advice
   D. seek and need to develop insight

6. Selma, a 9-year-old girl, an only child, I.Q. 105, has recently become irritable, restless, and unable to sit still. Her handwriting has deteriorated and her school work in general has fallen off. Medical examination indicates that she has a rheumatic heart condition. Her mother thinks she is lazy and should be made to work harder on her homework. Her father thinks his wife is too strict, and they often contradict each other's orders to Selma. On the basis of the information given, the psychologist is most justified in judging that Selma's behavior is   6.____

   A. an indication of chorea resulting from a rheumatic infection
   B. an indication of increasing emotional tension resulting from the dissension between the parents

C. primarily due to a rheumatic condition, but aggravated by the parental disagreement
D. primarily caused by worries of an origin not yet disclosed

7. In the application of his technique of play therapy, David M. Levy stressed the use of

   A. construction toys
   B. plastic materials
   C. dolls representing the family pattern
   D. group activities with other children of the same maturity level

8. The functions of a visiting teacher resemble MOST closely the functions of the

   A. exchange professor   B. hospital intern
   C. remedial teacher   D. social worker

9. To reduce vocalization in silent reading, it is BEST to

   A. pay no attention to it as the pupils will outgrow it in time
   B. have the pupils read easy material rapidly for the thought
   C. give the pupils material to read that is so difficult as to absorb their full attention
   D. make the pupils aware of the necessity for avoiding lip movement during reading

10. The MOST serious objection to using standardized social studies tests to evaluate pupil achievement is that the

   A. published social studies tests are admittedly tests of factual information
   B. score is influenced unduly by the size of the pupil's vocabulary
   C. scoring keys generally allow too much scope to the teacher's subjective judgment
   D. social studies courses of studies vary considerably from one locality to another

11. The Compass Diagnostic Tests are applicable to which one of the following subjects?

   A. Arithmetic   B. Composition
   C. Penmanship   D. Spelling

12. The Betts Keystone Telebinocular Tests are designed to measure

   A. eye-hand coordination   B. fixation time
   C. size of recognition span   D. visual functioning

13. Which one of the following names is NOT associated with a reading readiness test?

   A. Gates   B. Gray
   C. Metropolitan   D. Monroe

14. A diagnostic handwriting scale has been prepared by

   A. Ayres   B. Freeman   C. Pintner   D. Thorndike

15. Of the following tests of spelling ability, the one that provides a test task that resembles MOST closely the normal functional situation in spelling is the

   A. Ayres   B. Metropolitan
   C. Monroe   D. Morrison-McCall

16. An outstanding book on disability in speech has been written by

A. A.I. Gates B. J. Harris
C. L.E. Travis D. Seashore

17. A metronoscope is a device for

    A. exposing strips of reading material for drill purposes
    B. developing even rhythm in such subjects as music and typewriting
    C. transmuting speech sounds into a visual record
    D. recording the speed and character of eye movements

18. Personality inventories have been criticized on the ground that the introspective report of the subject cannot be relied upon. The MOST cogent rebuttal of this criticism is that

    A. many of the inventories have employed empirical means of determining the significance of each response
    B. there is no other approach, basically, to the determination of personality
    C. many items on widely used tests of judgment and appreciation are equally subjective
    D. the defect is not inherent since the inventories can be perfected by the elimination of non-factual items

19. Which of the following tests or scales of art ability requires the drawing of a picture on a blank sheet of paper?

    A. Kline-Carey B. Lewerenz
    C. McAdory D. Meier

20. Which one of the following psychologists has developed a scale of so'cial maturity?

    A. Doll B. Healy C. Pintner D. Woodworth

21. The sociogram as developed by Moreno is concerned with the

    A. diagrammatic expression of spontaneously evolved dramatic plots
    B. picturization of inter-personal preferences
    C. rating of social distance among nationality groups
    D. plotting of trends in public opinion polls

22. A report on a child who was referred for study of his educational disabilities includes the statement that he makes many "reversals". This signifies that he tends to

    A. substitute one sound for another
    B. shift from hand to hand in different activities
    C. read words backwards
    D. revert to a backward slant in writing

23. Which of the following names is NOT associated with a book on child development?

    A. Gesell B. Jersild C. McCall D. Brooks

24. According to recent writers on the subject, the main distinction between planning instruction for the deaf and for the hard of hearing arises from the fact that in the case of the deaf

    A. the handicap is present prior to the acquisition of speech
    B. the hearing loss is greater

C. the defect has an innate rather than an acquired origin
D. nerve injury as distinguished from bone or eardrum injury is involved

25. The activity program through its emphasis on learning by doing, is intended to make what use of intellectual processes?

    A. Stress them
    B. Include them
    C. Eliminate them
    D. Verbalize them

26. The Teacher's Word Book is a useful reference work because it

    A. lists the frequency of misspelling of the common words in the language
    B. indicates the words most often used by pupils at various chronological age levels
    C. notes the most commonly used meanings of the more frequently used words in the language
    D. provides a criterion for evaluating the vocabulary used in readers and school textbooks

27. The kind of elementary school boy who is MOST likely to be referred by a principal for study by a child guidance clinic is the pupil who

    A. misbehaves in the classroom
    B. does not have many close friendships with other children of his age
    C. is not interested in girls
    D. rarely volunteers in class

28. One of the fifth grade teachers in the school tells you that she is very much interested in diagnostic testing and remedial instruction, especially in arithmetic, but that her principal is reluctant to purchase the diagnostic tests she wishes to use with her pupils. As you speak with the teacher, you should explain that

    A. the arithmetic papers used in her class are a fruitful source of material that she can analyze for diagnostic purposes
    B. she can examine these diagnostic tests at any college or university library and make her own mimeographed copies of this test
    C. you will tell the principal of her needs and see that he orders the tests she wishes to have
    D. teachers are sufficiently well paid to purchase these tests out of their own pockets

29. A junior high school mathematics teacher complains that although her pupils seem to understand each new process as she explains it to them and get good marks in the tests she administers at the end of each unit of work, they generally do poorly on the examinations administered at the end of the term.
Of the following, the MOST helpful suggestion a psychologist can give the teacher is to suggest that she

    A. explain to her class that pupils who do not pass in the final examinations cannot be advanced to the next grade
    B. improve the way in which she motivates her initial lesson
    C. organize an honor roll in mathematics so that the good pupils will get the social commendation they deserve
    D. provide for overlearning by spaced repetitions through regular drill and reviews

30. As you have lunch with some of the teachers at the elementary school to which you have been assigned on a testing project, you sense that they regard the assignment of school psychologist as just one more illustration of a tendency to coddle pupils. They tell you quite frankly that the money spent on psychologists could be spent more wisely in appointing more teachers and thus reducing class size. In order to help win these teachers over to a better understanding of the contribution which school psychologists make, you should indicate how

    A. little the salaries paid to all the school psychologists in the city would contribute to solving the problem of reducing class size
    B. inadequate is the information that teachers have about the emotional lives of pupils
    C. school psychologists can help teachers in the solution of the school problems
    D. exacting and time consuming is the work done by the school psychologists

30.____

31. When classroom teachers attempt to deal with children's emotional difficulties which are at the basis of much serious misconduct, they are inclined to

    A. plan treatment programs which cover too long a period of time
    B. stress the removal of the cause rather than the elimination of annoying symptoms
    C. deal with immediate rather than basic causes of misconduct
    D. spend too much time assembling unnecessary data

31.____

32. A high school teacher of economics in an academic high school tells you that almost half of the pupils in his senior year classes spend most of their time in his class, daydreaming rather than participating in the class lesson. The MOST promising procedure for this teacher to follow is to

    A. refer these daydreaming pupils to the Bureau of Child Guidance for intensive study
    B. realize that daydreaming is normal among adolescents
    C. base his lessons on economic problems confronting his pupils
    D. administer short surprise quizzes whenever inattention becomes widespread

32.____

33. In the course of a series of counseling interviews, a six-teen-year-old high school senior whose school record has been very successful, remarks: "I'm just a failure. Marks don't mean anything. I know I don't have any brains.
    When it comes to doing anything that amounts to something, I'm not much good!" If you, as a psychologist, were following the counseling method of Carl R. Rogers, an appropriate comment to make at this point would be:

    A. "You feel you don't amount to much in the things that count."
    B. "What you say shows that you are suffering from an inferiority complex."
    C. "Would you like me to give you an intelligence test?"
    D. "A lot of people feel that way at your age; you'll snap out of it."

33.____

34. A psychologist is justified in recommending the keeping of anecdotal records by a teacher because they

    A. increase learning by lending interest to lessons
    B. improve the pupils' oral expression by means of a natural medium
    C. provide a break in the tension that often accompanies school work
    D. yield a valuable account of pupil behavior

34.____

35. A child who is being tested for possible placement in a CRMD class is found to have a Stanford-Binet I.Q. of 73 with very little scatter. The psychologist knows that the probable error of an I.Q. in this range is about 3 points. He should recommend that the child

    A. need not be re-examined, since his I.Q. will not change more than three points
    B. need not be re-examined, since his I.Q. will more probably drop rather than rise
    C. should be re-examined, because the chances are 50 in 100 that his I.Q. will rise more than three points
    D. should be re-examined because there is one chance in four that his I.Q. will rise more than three points

36. Experimental reports on the transfer of training indicate that the degree of transfer varies with the intelligence of pupils

    A. not at all
    B. slightly
    C. to a great extent
    D. inversely

37. The principle of the conditioned response as formulated by E.L. Thorndike was referred to as the law of

    A. associative shifting
    B. recency
    C. exercise
    D. readiness

38. Egocentricity, irritability, selfishness and moroseness are MOST characteristic of which one of the following personality types?

    A. Paranoid
    B. Epileptoid
    C. Cycloid
    D. Schizoid

39. Which of the following has been shown in the laboratory to result in loss of critical ability, including the capacity for self-criticism?

    A. Aphasia
    B. Aphonia
    C. Ataxia
    D. Anoxia

40. Studies of SUCCESSFUL foster homes point to the conclusion that the discipline in such homes tends to be

    A. lenient
    B. strict
    C. consistent
    D. self-imposed

41. According to studies of the success of foster home placement, which of the following combinations of factors is most likely to be associated with successful placement?

    A. Under nine years of age at placement, and average intelligence
    B. Over thirteen years of age at placement, and very superior intelligence
    C. Under nine years of age at placement, and very superior mentality
    D. Over thirteen years of age at placement, and average mentality

42. The MAJOR innovation which the organization of child guidance clinics introduced in the treatment of problem behavior was the provision it made for

    A. adequate psychometric study of each child
    B. educating teachers to a realization of the part they must play in the prevention and correction of emotional problems
    C. treating the cause rather than the symptoms of maladjustment
    D. pooling the resources of psychologists, psychiatrists, pediatricians and social workers

43. Psychobiology is MOST closely associated with the name of

    A. Alfred Adler
    B. Clifford Beers
    C. Adolf Meyer
    D. John B. Watson

44. As part of a group study of a special opportunity class, a psychologist wants to include a quick method of determining the social relationships existing within the class. Of the following procedures, the one which is BEST adapted to this purpose is

    A. a group Rorschach test
    B. the Pintner Aspects of Personality
    C. systematic observations by the psychologist in the classroom
    D. a sociogram based on a "Guess Who" questionnaire

45. Which of the following pairs does NOT represent an accurate association:

    A. Beck-Rorschach test
    B. Stern-Cloud pictures
    C. Jung-Ward association
    D. Koffka-Visual Motor Gestalt test

46. In the "therapeutic group" described by S.R.Slavson in his "Creative Group Therapy," the aim of the leader is to

    A. release the tensions within the children by developing creative artistic expression
    B. set a model of behavior for the children to follow
    C. develop the gradual growth of healthy relationships
    D. achieve emotional stability through wholesome physical activity

47. The CAVD test of the intellect was originated by

    A. Burt   B. Spearman   C. Thurstone   D. Thorndike

48. Which one of the following tests or pairs of tests does NOT yield non-language as well as language I.Q.'s? The

    A. Pintner-Durost
    B. Pintner Intermediate
    C. California
    D. Otis Self-Administering

49. On which one of the following tests of the Wechsler-Belle-vue Scales is partial credit allowed for the individual items or tasks?

    A. General Information
    B. General Comprehension
    C. Arithmetical Reasoning
    D. Picture Completion

50. Two different responses to the question as to the similarity between wood and alcohol on the Wechsler-Bellevue are: (1) "Both are useful"; (2) "Alcohol comes from wood". 50.____

    A. Both responses receive a credit of 2.
    B. The first response receives a credit of 2, while the second response receives a credit of 0.
    C. The first response receives a credit of 0, while the second response receives a credit of 2.
    D. Both responses receive a credit of 0.

KEY (CORRECT ANSWERS)

1. D	11. A	21. B	31. C	41. A
2. C	12. D	22. C	32. C	42. D
3. C	13. B	23. C	33. A	43. C
4. C	14. B	24. A	34. D	44. D
5. A	15. C	25. B	35. D	45. D
6. C	16. C	26. D	36. C	46. C
7. C	17. A	27. A	37. A	47. D
8. D	18. A	28. A	38. B	48. D
9. B	19. A	29. D	39. D	49. B
10. D	20. A	30. C	40. C	50. D

EXAMINATION SECTION
TEST 1

DIRECTIONS: Each question or incomplete statement is followed by several suggested answers or completions. Select the one that *BEST* answers the question or completes the statement. *PRINT THE LETTER OF THE CORRECT ANSWER IN THE SPACE AT THE RIGHT.*

1. The feature considered MOST responsible for therapeutic improvement in the major psychotherapeutic system is

    A. intellectual insight
    B. interpersonal interaction
    C. deep interpretation
    D. persistence in application of appropriate theory

2. A report about a 15-year-old girl to the school psychologist indicates that she is involved in "conjoint family therapy."
   This *most likely* indicates that

    A. every member in the family is in some form of individual or group therapy with a different therapist
    B. she and her parents see the same therapist but at different times
    C. she and her siblings have the same therapist but the parents are seen by a social worker
    D. all family members are seen as a group by the same therapist

3. The perceptions of the client from his own frame of reference are called

    A. gestalt therapy   B. logotherapy
    C. phenomenology   D. paradigmatic

4. The basic re-learning process which is present in most forms of psychotherapy is MOST frequently attributed to the

    A. strong self-punitive aspects involved in interpretation
    B. catharsis
    C. reinforcement of the defense mechanisms
    D. extinction of the defenses and development of new insights

5. In psychotherapy, especially in psychoanalysis, the patient frequently perceives the therapist in different roles and images.
   This phenomenon is called

    A. resistance   B. libido
    C. transference   D. cognitive style

6. The term "desensitization" is used to refer to a process in

    A. psychoanalytic psychotherapy in working through body image problems
    B. special education procedures for psychotic children
    C. conditioning therapy in reducing anxiety
    D. the Rankian method for treatment of separation anxiety

7. Behavior therapy as a mode of behavior modification tends to focus upon 7.___

   A. the prior sequence of experience that has established current habits
   B. present behavior and its consequences
   C. the helplessness of the patient in his current circumstances
   D. the emotions as the cause of the patient's difficulties

8. Intensive study of male delinquents has shown that many serious personality problems underlie their *acting-out* behavior. Basic to these problems is an indication that 8.___

   A. brain dysrhythmia plays an important role
   B. prolonged early separations from parents have damaged capacity for object relations
   C. excessive exposure to other delinquents has seduced them into anti-social acts
   D. corporal punishment has resulted in an indifferent attitude to authority

9. The estimated frequency of mental deficiency in the peoples of Western civilization is approximately 9.___

   A. 2%   B. 4%   C. 6%   D. 8%

10. School phobia is MOST commonly found in which one of the following? 10.___

    A. Kindergarten   B. Intermediate grades
    C. Lower elementary grades D. K-6 grades

11. School phobia is generally viewed as a fear of 11.___

    A. the teacher   B. rejection by peers
    C. failure in school D. leaving mother

12. Which of the following statements is LEAST accurate with respect to defense or behavior mechanisms? 12.___

    A. They are unconscious
    B. While they may be an expression of maladjustment, they also provide stability
    C. Of all behavior, that stemming from the action of defense mechanisms is most modifiable through rational explanation
    D. Defense mechanisms can be part of normal behavior

13. Discrepancies between the attitudes of the classroom teacher and the clinician toward problem behavior arise MAINLY because the 13.___

    A. teacher lacks the understanding of the dynamics of the pupils' emotional life
    B. teacher considers withdrawn and non-aggressive children to be good pupils
    C. clinicians have deeper insights into the psychology of children
    D. clinicians and teachers have different roles

14. Girls are usually better adjusted than boys in the school milieu because 14.___

    A. teachers generally lack the sophistication to understand boys' methods of adjustment
    B. teachers' expectations are more rigorous and demanding for boys than for girls
    C. teachers generally underestimate the boys' capabilities which disillusions boys and encourages them to rebel
    D. teachers tend to value behaviors which are more characteristic of girls than of boys

15. In psychoanalytic theory, the selection of the defense mechanism is a function of the

   A. ego   B. id   C. superego   D. libido

16. There are many factors involved in the development of a homosexual process in a boy. The LEAST likely factor to be at the root of the problem is

   A. experience only with men
   B. physiological disturbance
   C. severe disappointment in relation to his mother
   D. an intense longing to be loved by the father

17. A psychologist trying to establish specific age norms for a battery of commonly used projective techniques obtains permission from parents and school administrator to administer the tests to a large sample of high school students. He makes no promise to reveal the test results. After administering the tests and analyzing the data he finds that several students are on the verge of serious disturbance. With whom would he be ethically obliged to discuss the results of such students' tests? The

   A. parents   B. student's teacher
   C. student   D. school administrator

18. With regard to the effect of mixed dominance on reading achievement, summaries of research to date show that

   A. there is a high relationship between mixed dominance and reading retardation
   B. there is no relationship between mixed dominance and reading retardation
   C. the relationship between mixed dominance and reading retardation is controversial
   D. mixed dominance affects word recognition only in brain injured children

19. Of the following, the symptom which is LEAST likely to be characteristic of the hard-of-hearing child is

   A. listlessness and inattentiveness
   B. poor oral reading ability
   C. low-pitched voice quality
   D. louder-than-necessary voice volume

20. Of the following, the symptom which is LEAST often present among brain damaged children is

   A. hyperactivity   B. mental deficiency
   C. motor incoordination   D. apathy

21. For J.B. Watson, all fears – except the fears of falling and of loud noises – are learned in accordance with the principles of

   A. trial and error learning   B. operant conditioning
   C. Pavlovian conditioning   D. Thorndikean connectionism

22. The child develops an ideal self-concept through

   A. learning   B. maturation
   C. discipline   D. perceptual discrimination

23. The projective technique which has been used MOST often in the study of the mentally retarded is the

   A. Rorschach
   B. TAT
   C. HTP
   D. Mosaics

24. Intelligence test scores between siblings show a correlation of about

   A. -.50
   B. .00
   C. +.0
   D. +.50

25. At all stages of growth, physical development is an important factor in the individual's adjustment. It has been found that

   A. early maturing girls and late maturing boys have MORE adjustment difficulties than late maturing girls and early maturing boys
   B. early maturing girls and late maturing boys have FEWER adjustment difficulties than late maturing girls and early maturing boys
   C. early maturing girls and early maturing boys have MORE adjustment difficulties than late maturing girls and late maturing boys
   D. late maturing girls and late maturing boys have the SAME adjustment difficulties as early maturing girls and early maturing boys

26. Of the following, the one which would stress an educational program based on classical behaviorism is

   A. conditioning
   B. understanding
   C. thinking
   D. volitional activity

27. B.F. Skinner's data on learning stress

   A. operant conditioning
   B. Pavlovian conditioning
   C. deductive behaviorism
   D. descriptive behavior

28. The factor which is generally considered the MOST important requisite for learning is

   A. a democratic environment
   B. an accepting teacher
   C. a motivated student
   D. acceptance by peers

29. A response made while an individual is anxious will *most likely* become habitual if it

   A. produces no additional anxiety
   B. converts the anxiety to fear
   C. strengthens the anxiety
   D. lessens the anxiety

30. Rating of IQ on the Goodenough Harris Draw-a-Man test performed by prepubertals tends to be

   A. the same for boys and girls
   B. unrelated to IQs obtained on standard intelligence scales
   C. superior for girls
   D. superior for boys

31. In terms of developed body language principles, the head of a human figure drawn represents 31.____

   A. a concrete self-portrait of the person who drew the figure
   B. the area relating to motor, aggressive and/or sexual acting out
   C. the part that is usually most difficult to execute
   D. the area relating to intellect, sensitivity, passivity, and/or control

32. The correlation between measures of intelligence and measures of creativity is 32.____

   A. Insignificant over the entire range of IQ scores
   B. low but significant if the group tested is in the high IQ range
   C. negligible if the group tested is in the high IQ range
   D. low but significant if the group tested is in the low IQ range

33. The scores of a large group of adults on a test of musical aptitude and a test of mechanical comprehension yield a correlation of -.50. Of the following, the CORRECT inference is that 33.____

   A. persons who obtain relatively high scores on one test tend to get low scores on the other
   B. musical aptitudes and mechanical comprehension are not related to one another
   C. most people are relatively low on both musical aptitude and mechanical comprehension
   D. an individual cannot have high scores or low scores on both tests

34. In standardization of tests the coefficient of equivalence is a measure of 34.____

   A. reliability   B. predictability
   C. validity   D. stability

35. In statistical terms the expression of a perfect relationship between two variables is stated as a coefficient of correlation equal to 35.____

   A. .00   B. +.50   C. 1.00   D. 50

36. Which one of the following is LEAST likely to be indicative of color shock on the Rorschach? 36.____

   A. Significant delay prior to the first scorable response to Card VIII
   B. A total production of 3 responses to the last 3 cards in a complete record of 22 responses
   C. FC responses to Cards III, VIII and X
   D. F responses to Cards I, V, VI and VII only

37. A nine-year-old boy who has been in this country for one year, having come from El Salvador, is referred because he does not like to play with other children and because he becomes very angry with the teacher whenever she tells him what to do. In the initial testing, the psychologist, to obtain the best estimate of the child's mental level, should administer the 37.____

   A. Wechsler Intelligence Scale for Children
   B. Kuhlmann-Binet
   C. Cornell-Coxe Scale
   D. Rorschach

38. An interest inventory yields three separate scores which have the following statistics: 38.___

Reliability		Intercorrelations	
Score I	.76	Score I vs II	.60
Score II	.81	Score I vs III	.40
Score III	.79	Score II vs III	.20

Which pair of scores would yield the GREATEST amount of diagnostic or differential information?

    A. I and II   B. I and III   C. II and III
    D. More information is needed to answer the question

39. Guthrie would contend that learning is an 39.___

    A. S-S process dependent on contiguity
    B. S-S process dependent on reinforcement
    C. S-R process dependent on contiguity
    D. S-R process dependent on reinforcement

40. The reinforcement schedule that typically maintains the gambling of human beings Is 40.___

    A. fixed-interval   B. fixed-ratio
    C. variable-interval   D. variable-ratio

41. The tendency to respond to a stimulus similar to, but not identical with, the original stimulus used in a learning experience is termed 41.___

    A. acquisition   B. spontaneous recovery
    C. extinction   D. generalization

42. Hebb's theories about the functioning of the nervous system suggest that there is a great difference between the learning of 42.___

    A. signs and solutions   B. males and females
    C. acts and movements   D. children and adults

43. In Pavlovian conditioning, extinction of a conditioned reflex is produced by presenting the 43.___

    A. conditioned stimulus but not the unconditioned stimulus
    B. unconditioned stimulus but not the conditioned stimulus
    C. conditioned and unconditioned stimuli together
    D. conditioned stimulus followed by a pain-producing stimulus

44. Children who are taller and heavier than their age-mates at age two, tend, when they become adults, to have height and weight that is 44.___

    A. below average
    B. above average
    C. average
    D. unpredictable from two-year status

45. The practice of reinforcing responses that are closer and closer approximations to the behavior one is trying to teach is called 45.___

    A. discrimination learning   B. branching
    C. shaping   D. respondent conditioning

46. Contiguity theorists reject the view that learning

    A. is a continuous process
    B. consists of S-R associations
    C. requires reinforcement
    D. can be distinguished from performance

47. Learning curves indicate a basic relationship between the variables of

    A. time and work
    B. trial and error
    C. positive and negative acceleration
    D. distraction and application

48. Dullness, autism, thought disturbance and gradual decline of activity is MOST characteristic of which one of the following?

    A. A depression
    B. A schizophrenic reaction
    C. An acute neurotic reaction
    D. A severe physical exhaustion and need for rest

49. Most frequently associated with delinquency and antisocial behavior is

    A. distortion of the ego
    B. excessive ideational perserveration
    C. lack of will power
    D. distortion of the superego

50. Stutterers tend to be different from other speech-disordered children in that they

    A. are normal or above-average in intelligence as a group
    B. are below-average in intelligence as a group
    C. have a higher degree of damage to the nervous system
    D. have parents who show little anxiety and pressure for mastery

KEY (CORRECT ANSWERS)

1. B	11. D	21. B	31. D	41. D
2. D	12. C	22. A	32. C	42. D
3. B	13. D	23. A	33. A	43. A
4. D	14. D	24. D	34. A	44. B
5. B	15. A	25. A	35. C	45. B
6. C	16. B	26. A	36. C	46. C
7. B	17. D	27. A	37. C	47. A
8. B	18. C	28. B	38. C	48. B
9. A	19. C	29. D	39. C	49. D
10. B	20. D	30. C	40. D	50. A

TEST 2

DIRECTIONS: Each question or incomplete statement is followed by several suggested answers or completions. Select the one that *BEST* answers the question or completes the statement. *PRINT THE LETTER OF THE CORRECT ANSWER IN THE SPACE AT THE RIGHT.*

1. A distribution of measurements is as follows:
   10, 9, 9, 8, 6, 5, 4, 4, 4, 4, 3
   The mode of this distribution is

   A. 4   B. 5   C. 6   D. 7

2. Within a given standardization group, a standard score (i.e. a z score) of 3.0 can BEST be characterized as

   A. below average   B. above average
   C. average   D. well above average

3. When identical scores are made on successive administrations of a measuring instrument, that instrument is said to be

   A. valid   B. reliable
   C. predictive   D. objective

4. In a normal distribution, a score which falls 2 standard deviations below the mean MOST closely approximates the

   A. first decile   B. third decile
   C. second decile   D. fourth decile

5. The cognitive function MOST sensitive to disturbance in a boy's psychological health is

   A. verbal ability
   B. abstract reasoning
   C. manipulation of numerical symbols
   D. memory

6. Reluctance or fear of attending school may appear at any age including adolescence. When it occurs in adolescence it should be treated

   A. in the same manner as that of a six year old
   B. as an anxiety-hysteria expected to yield successfully in six months
   C. as a serious disorder of the character structure and planned as a long-term therapy case
   D. directly with the expectancy of improvement in a short time

7. Geraldine, who is 5 years old, is described as in need of therapy but lacking in verbal skills. Given these circumstances, the *most likely* form of psychotherapy should be

   A. play therapy   B. hymnotherapy
   C. group therapy   D. speech therapy

8. The ability of delay gratification is a function of that part of the personality structure called the

   A. id   B. superego
   C. ego   D. preconscious

9. Studies of the outcome of mental disorder suggest that one of the causes of less favorable prognosis for the lower socio-economic group is

   A. their antagonism towards psychiatric treatment
   B. their reliance upon the advice of quacks
   C. persistent nutritional deficiencies
   D. reluctance on the part of psychiatrists to prescribe expensive drugs or somatic therapies

10. To achieve better care of patients in mental hospitals, the Joint Commission on Mental Illness and Health has recommended that

    A. bigger and better mental hospitals be constructed
    B. mental hospitals be integrated into the community
    C. intensive individual psychotherapeutic approaches be utilized to a greater extent
    D. new tranquilizing drugs be utilized in conjunction with psychotherapy

11. The law of effect states that a response will be strengthened if it is

    A. followed by reward
    B. based on insight
    C. exercised frequently
    D. rarely punished

12. B.F. Skinner regarded his teaching machine as superior to a human teacher because it could

    A. teach without the necessity of providing practice
    B. punish incorrect reponses as soon as they are made
    C. react without emotion to all of the learner's responses
    D. provide immediate reinforcement after a correct response

13. Responses mediated by the autonomic nervous system—such as salivation, perspiration, and pupillary contraction—can be elicited by "neutral" stimuli In accordance with the principles of

    A. trial and error learning
    B. operant conditioning
    C. rote learning
    D. Pavlovian conditioning

14. Studies of learning sets suggest that insightful learning, when it occurs, is based on

    A. motives that are stronger than is usually the case
    B. the ability to learn without reinforcement
    C. rapid attainment of homeostatic equilibrium
    D. extensive experience with similar problems

15. In learning theory terms, the psychoanalytic mechanism of displacement may be seen as an illustration of

    A. reinforcement
    B. extinction
    C. discrimination
    D. generalization

16. A comparison of the learning curves of rapid and slow learners, in which correct responses are plotted against time, indicates that the

    A. curves for rapid and slow learners rise at the same rate, but the slow learners level off more sharply
    B. curve for rapid learners drops less sharply and levels off more slowly
    C. curve for rapid learners rises more sharply and levels off more rapidly
    D. curve for rapid learners drops more sharply and levels off more rapidly

17. A teacher of commercial subjects describes four approaches that he might use in the teaching of typewriting. Which one of the following four approaches does the weight of the available evidence suggest is MOST productive?

    A. Trial and error learning without guidance whenever possible
    B. Allow errors to appear, and then correct them
    C. Concentrate guidance in the early phases of learning
    D. Concentrate guidance in the later stages of learning, where the student sees his need for help

18. Client-centered therapy is PRIMARILY directed toward

    A. probing basic motivational patterns
    B. counseling on the basis of psychological tests
    C. uncovering early childhood experiences
    D. stimulating self insight

19. The non-directive interview is effective with children because it

    A. gives the child a feeling of being understood
    B. disguises prying
    C. permits the teacher to give advice without being punitive
    D. prevents the child from feeling guilty

20. Of the following, which is the MOST correct statement concerning the most frequently found type of mental defective?

    A. He falls in the moron or borderline classification
    B. He has grown up in a normal cultural setting
    C. He will not be able to care for himself without help
    D. He shows abnormal EEG tracings

21. Compared with children without speech defects, children with speech defects, excluding stutterers, tend to be

    A. retarded intellectually
    B. different in kind from the children of normal speech
    C. increasingly adjusted as they mature
    D. physically handicapped in other ways

22. The incidence of mental illness among the mentally deficient appears to be

    A. lower than in the general population
    B. much higher than in the general population

C. about the same as in the general population
D. unpredictably related to that of the general population

23. When compared with normal children, intellectually gifted children are, on the average, 23._____

    A. physically superior
    B. subject to more eye defects
    C. frailer
    D. clumsy physically

24. The rate of juvenile delinquency tends to be highest in those areas of a city in which there is a great deal of 24._____

    A. police observation
    B. social disorganization
    C. commercial activity
    D. educational pressure

25. Which of the following symptoms is NOT characteristic of the preschizophrenic child? 25._____

    A. seclusiveness
    B. regression
    C. physical inactivity
    D. elaborate symbolic language

26. When an illness is described as psychosomatic, it means that the symptoms 26._____

    A. are psychological, but physiological factors contribute
    B. are physiological, but psychological factors contribute
    C. and all contributing factors are psychological
    D. and all contributing factors are physiological

27. Most pronounced cases of bullying and aggressiveness are the result of efforts on the child's part to 27._____

    A. impress adults with his strength
    B. gain the attention of those around him
    C. reach a level of achievement that is beyond him
    D. compensate for deep feelings of inadequacy

28. Aubrey has applied for several college scholarships, but has not obtained any. He says that none of the colleges really examines the candidates carefully or fairly. Which defense mechanism is he manifesting? 28._____

    A. rationalization
    B. sublimation
    C. projection
    D. repression

29. When a person says, "I am so fond of you," when you know he actually dislikes you, there is reason to suspect that he is using the defense mechanism of 29._____

    A. introjection
    B. rationalization
    C. projection
    D. reaction formation

30. According to Hall and Lindsey, the MOST important indicator of the fruitfulness or value of a personality theory is 30._____

    A. the extent to which it is a general theory of behavior rather than a single-domain theory
    B. that it generates significant research

C. that it is purposive (or teleological) rather than "mechanistic"
D. the extent to which it deals with the learning process

31. The theorist who rejects the importance of studying the "total individual" is

    A. Murphy   B. Goldstein   C. Eysenck   D. Rogers

32. A theory of personality which stresses the lack of continuity in development and the relative independence of the functioning adult from the events of childhood or infancy is that of

    A. Allport   B. Freud   C. Miller   D. Sullivan

33. Of the theoreticians listed below, which one is MOST closely associated with the concept of syncretic thinking?

    A. Arnold Gesell   B. Jean Piaget
    C. Harry Stack Sullivan   D. Sigmund Freud

34. In Freud's formulation, however dissimilar neurotic symptoms may be, they ALWAYS

    A. involve compulsions
    B. are unconscious
    C. yield a degree of satisfaction
    D. are recognizable

35. As contrasted with children of the middle class, the lower class child tends to experience

    A. few anxieties over "good" and "bad" behavior
    B. deeper repression of aggressive and sexual impulses
    C. less physical enjoyment of normal body functions
    D. greater needs to achieve and excel

36. At the adolescent level, "adjustment" usually depends MOST strongly on having

    A. acceptance from peers
    B. adequate sex education
    C. average school achievement or better
    D. warm approval from teachers

37. The fantasies of a child are MOST often used by a psychologist as a clue to his

    A. level of maturity   B. social adjustment
    C. inner needs   D. intelligence

38. The listless, apathetic behavior of children reared in foundling homes is MOST often

    A. generally poor heredity   B. environmental crowding
    C. deprivation of love   D. inadequate diet

39. Of the following self-concepts, the MOST desirable one for a child to develop from the standpoint of mental health is:

    A. Whatever I do is good
    B. If I fail at something, It isn't important
    C. I am capable of reaching my goals
    D. I must always be alert to my weaknesses

40. Of the following, which is the MOST accurate statement concerning the effect of inherited biological characteristics? They

    A. determine the course of personality development
    B. account for the resemblances of Individuals to their parents in aspects of emotional adjustment
    C. set certain limits to the potentialities of the individual for personality development
    D. play a major role in governing an Individual's behavior in conflict-producing situations

41. The latency period is a developmental state distinguished by

    A. no change
    B. rapid changes
    C. slow changes
    D. dramatic changes

42. Virtually all of the 6000 citizens in a mining community earn less than $5000 per year. However, a few of them, the factory owners, earn as much as nearly all the workers combined. The measure of central tendency which would give the MOST accurate picture of the economic level of the whole community is the

    A. arithmetic mean
    B. median
    C. mode
    D. geometric mean

43. The Kuder-Richardson approach will give rise to a test reliability estimate that has essentially the same meaning as that obtained through the use of an odd-even approach when the

    A. test to which it is applied is speeded
    B. test items are homogeneous
    C. test items show a wide variation in difficulty
    D. standardization population shows a normal distribution in ability

44. The reliability of a difference between a score on Test A and a score on Test B is dependent upon the correlation between Test A and Test B, and upon the

    A. reliability of Test A and that of Test B
    B. range of scores on Test A and Test B
    C. absolute difference between the score on Test A and that of Test B
    D. standard deviations of Test A and Test B

45. A sample that is chosen in such a way as to guarantee to each member an equal probability of selection is USUALLY referred to as a

    A. random sample
    B. purposive sample
    C. reliable sample
    D. stratified sample

46. The reliability of a test may be estimated by comparing the results from the first half of the test with the results from the second half of the same test. This type of reliability is called

    A. internal consistency
    B. retest stability
    C. equivalent forms
    D. parallel forms

47. When an investigator uses a theory to set up hypotheses about what causes a person to get a certain test score he is using a type of validity called

   A. content
   B. concurrent
   C. predictive
   D. construct

48. In writing an anecdotal record which is to go into a pupil's cumulative record folder, the report should

   A. emphasize the teacher's reaction to the pupil
   B. describe the behavior of the pupil
   C. point out the pupil's personal problems
   D. be an interpretation of the present incident in the light of earlier contacts with the pupil

49. The development of local norms for use with a standardized achievement test battery is

   A. desirable, because each school needs to know how it stands in relation to other groups
   B. desirable, because this makes it easy to compare each individual with his own group
   C. undesirable, because it encourages a narrow, local orientation
   D. undesirable, because the national norms are the relevant yardsticks for most programs

50. The mean age in months for two groups of nursery school children was reported as 25.5. The standard deviation for group A was 3.4 and for group B it was 4.9. From this we may conclude that

   A. group A is more variable than group B
   B. that median age for group B is higher than for group A
   C. the age range of group B is greater than the age range in group A
   D. the measure of central tendency for group B is larger than for group A

KEY (CORRECT ANWSWERS)

1. A	11. A	21. A	31. C	41. B
2. D	12. D	22. B	32. A	42. C
3. C	13. D	23. A	33. C	43. B
4. A	14. D	24. C	34. C	44. A
5. C	15. D	25. D	35. A	45. A
6. C	16. C	26. B	36. A	46. A
7. A	17. C	27. D	37. B	47. D
8. B	18. D	28. A	38. B	48. B
9. A	19. A	29. D	39. C	49. B
10. B	20. A	30. B	40. C	50. C

TEST 3

DIRECTIONS: Each question or incomplete statement is followed by several suggested answers or completions. Select the one that BEST answers the question or completes the statement. PRINT THE LETTER OF THE CORRECT ANSWER IN THE SPACE AT THE RIGHT.

1. Which of the following should be considered the MOST important potential danger in the use of standardized achievement tests? 1._____

    A. They may fix the curriculum and focus attention on narrow objectives
    B. They may emphasize the failure of certain pupils
    C. They may interfere with the individualized treatment of pupils
    D. They may be misinterpreted by the general public

2. For which of the following tests would construct validity play the largest part in our evaluation of the instrument? 2._____

    A. A proficiency test for aviation mechanics
    B. A selection test designed to select sales persons
    C. An achievement test in high school social studies
    D. A test designed to appraise the trait of introversion

3. An I.Q. obtained on the 1960 revision of the Stanford-Binet Intelligence Scale is essentially 3._____

    A. an age score
    B. a standard score
    C. a grade score
    D. a percentile

4. The BEST indication of the validity of a test as a measure of aptitude for foreign language learning is the extent to which 4._____

    A. all children without foreign language training achieve the same score on the test
    B. scores on the test correlate with previous language training
    C. equal amounts of training In foreign language produce equal changes in test scores
    D. scores on the test at the beginning of the school year correlate with achievement

5. Which of the following procedures would ORDINARILY increase the reliability of a test? 5._____

    A. Increasing the number of people tested
    B. Increasing the time limit of the test
    C. Increasing the number of items on the test
    D. Increasing the homogeneity of the group tested

6. An individual's score on an achievement test is 75. The standard error of measurement for the test is reported to be 5 points. 6._____
What are the chances that the individual's TRUE SCORE is between 70 and 80?

    A. About 1 chance in 3
    B. About 2 chances in 3
    C. About 1 chance in 6
    D. About 2 chances in 9

7. The items on an achievement test were evaluated by subject matter specialists for importance and relevance to courses of study and teaching objectives. Which test characteristic is established by this procedure? 7._____

A. Statistical validity   B. Social utility
C. Content validity   D. Practicability

8. Which of the following skills is MOST frequently measured by means of a standardized product scale?

   A. arithmetic   B. spelling
   C. music   D. handwriting

9. The self-report inventory is probably MOST satisfactory when it is used to measure which of the following?

   A. Interest patterns
   B. Attitude toward communism
   C. Personal adjustment
   D. Character traits such as honesty

10. A recent development of importance in the construction of group intelligence tests is the

    A. combining of sub-tests into a single score
    B. selection of items on the basis of item analysis
    C. use of age norms instead of grade norms
    D. reporting of several specific scores in place of a single I.Q.

11. In determining test reliability, which of the following techniques will tend to give the LOWEST coefficient?

    A. Test-retest   B. Split-halves
    C. Comparable forms   D. Kuder-Richardson

12. Studies comparing scores on the Stanford-Binet and Wechsler scales indicate that brighter children tend to show

    A. higher scores on Wechsler
    B. higher scores on the Stanford-Binet
    C. equally high scores on both scales
    D. markedly different scores on the two scales, with no consistent pattern apparent

13. A test in which the items, whether through intent or accident, measure different traits will tend to

    A. have low internal consistency
    B. have a smaller standard deviation than other tests
    C. give rise to a high Kuder-Richardson coefficient
    D. provide an efficient estimate of ability

14. According to Thurstone, the PRIMARY mental abilities are

    A. abilities to perform widely differing tasks, which indicate level of an individual's intelligence because of their high intercorrelations
    B. completely independent special abilities contributing to intelligence
    C. relatively independent special abilities which make up intelligence
    D. a group of relatively independent aptitudes, one of which is intelligence

15. Of the following, the MOST difficult task in validating a test is

    A. defining one's objectives
    B. achieving a reliable measure
    C. determining internal consistency
    D. finding an adequate criterion

16. The "two-factor" theory of organization of intelligence was advanced by

    A. Thorndike   B. Spearman   C. Thurstone   D. Kelley

17. Standardized reading tests that are part of achievement test batteries are USUALLY

    A. silent reading tests   B. interest tests
    C. administered Individually   D. oral tests

18. One of the advantages of using standardized reading tests as compared with informal teacher-made tests in reading, is that standardized tests

    A. afford comparison of a pupil's achievement with that of others of similar age and grade placement
    B. permit analysis of error types
    C. emphasize the meaningful rather than the mechanical aspects of reading
    D. are more interesting and varied than Informal tests

19. Of the following kinds of reading tests, which would tend to have the HIGHEST correlation with verbal intelligence?

    A. Oral reading
    B. Phonic ability
    C. Silent reading comprehension
    D. Rate of reading

20. Which of the following factors in reading readiness is NOT measured by most reading readiness tests?

    A. Experiental background   B. Visual discrimination
    C. Word meanings   D. Interest in reading

21. Probably the GREATEST task for the typical child in Grade 1 to master in reading is

    A. the meanings of the words used in his readers
    B. the recognition and recall of the printed words
    C. the concepts behind the words in his readers
    D. the difficult sentence patterns used in his books

22. Which of the following statements regarding 1st grade children with Mental Ages below 6 1/2 is MOST acceptable in the light of present research findings on readiness?

    A. Reading should be delayed until an M.A. of 6 1/2 is reached
    B. They should be given a pre-reading program emphasizing speaking and listening before formal reading instruction is introduced
    C. They can learn to read if the beginning reading materials are easy enough
    D. They should have an additional year of kindergarten experience

23. Which of the following statements is the MOST valid regarding the use of reading readiness test scores?

    A. A teacher should not permit a child to read words if he scores below average on a readiness test
    B. A readiness test score below average should be analyzed further so that appropriate steps may be taken to develop readiness in specific areas of weakness
    C. Children with below average total readiness scores should be taken on trips to the zoo, park, and museums
    D. Children with total low readiness scores should participate in many language and play activities to build up their linguistic backgrounds

24. Many intelligence tests used in schools are unsuitable for use with reading disability cases because they

    A. are group tests
    B. require the child to answer questions
    C. are performance tests
    D. require the child to read the questions

25. Probably the MOST useful information for a teacher to determine in making a diagnosis of a child who has a reading problem is

    A. the underlying psychological problems
    B. parental attitudes towards his reading
    C. the grade level and specific strengths and weaknesses in reading
    D. the one definite cause of the reading problem

26. For the English speaking 2nd grade child of average intelligence, which of the following statements would be MOST correct?

    A. His reading-recognition vocabulary is greater than his speaking vocabulary
    B. His speaking vocabulary is more advanced than his reading-recognition vocabulary
    C. His reading and speaking vocabularies are about equal
    D. There is no consistency in the relation between his speaking vocabulary and his reading-recognition vocabulary

27. Roger is in the 5th grade. He is exactly ten years old. His Stanford-Binet IQ is 90 and he scored 3.1 on a standardized reading test given at the end of the 4th grade. His reading ability is

    A. below grade level but normal for his age
    B. below grade level but he is working up to his mental age expectancy
    C. below grade level and below normal for his mental ability
    D. retarded for his grade, but he does not have a reading disability

28. The major criticism of modern reading programs by such critics as Rudolf Flesch (Why Johnny Can't Read) and Charles Walcutt (Tomorrow's Illiterates) is that most of these programs

    A. do not expose the child to critical reading early enough
    B. do not give sufficient emphasis to the teaching of phonics
    C. do not have stories suitable for lower-class children
    D. have very dull stories

29. Which of the following is probably the BEST technique for judging the reading difficulty of a primary book?

    A. An informal textbook test
    B. An interest inventory
    C. The Gates Diagnostic
    D. The Spache Readability Formula

30. In selecting children for a remedial reading program which of the following would be the BEST criterion?

    A. Children who read two or more years below their grade placement
    B. Children whose reading ages are one or more years below their mental ages
    C. Poor readers with no emotional difficulties
    D. Children who need help with comprehension

31. Defining personality as "the end product of our habit systems" expresses a concept MOST characteristic of a psychological orientation termed

    A. behavioristic
    B. Gestalt
    C. psychoanalytic
    D. personalistic

32. The effect of adding information to first impressions of personality is that judgment becomes

    A. more accurate
    B. more confident but not necessarily more accurate
    C. confused with reduction in accuracy
    D. less accurate

33. Of the following processes or mechanisms, the one involving the GREATEST amount of consciousness is

    A. repression
    B. suppression
    C. identification
    D. projection

34. Studies on intelligence and creativity have yielded findings which indicate that

    A. the two characteristics are completely independent
    B. they are independent for subjects of high average ability and above
    C. they are negatively correlated
    D. for all practical purposes measuring one trait is essentially the same as measuring the other

35. According to Freud's notion of an instinct, the MOST variable feature is the

    A. aim   B. source   C. object   D. impetus

36. According to Freudian concepts the displaceability of energy early in life is due to the

    A. flexibility of the ego structure
    B. inability of the ID to form fine discrimination between objects
    C. immaturity of the perceptual process
    D. operation of the super-ego

37. Fromm's concept of the "marketing orientation" refers MOST immediately to

    A. a person's aptitude for commerce
    B. the undue value society places on competition
    C. treating personal attributes and values as commodities
    D. a person who is concerned with showing off

38. Gordon Allport is an important proponent of a psychology oriented toward a

    A. search for universal causes
    B. more rigorous quantification
    C. science rooted in the finding of psychopathology
    D. science of individuality

39. Which theorist discusses modern man as being free from many of the restrictions of more primitive times, without having the freedom to develop himself fully?

    A. Fromm   B. Lewin   C. Hull   D. Sullivan

40. Which one of the following is associated with a personality theory derived from factor analysis?

    A. Spearman   B. Lewin   C. Hull   D. Eysenck

41. A teacher tells you that one of her students had difficulty solving a problem and made errors. Suddenly, he exclaimed he had the answer. It was the correct one. Of the following, the psychologist whose theory of learning would be MOST helpful to her in understanding the process her pupil underwent is

    A. Koffka   B. Hull   C. Thorndike   D. Guthrie

42. Laboratory studies of induced neuroses in animals show that

    A. when the frustrating situations are removed, the animals' neurotic behavior disappears
    B. animals have a lower tolerance than humans to frustrating situations
    C. a single type of reaction to frustrating situations results
    D. most induced neurotic behavior in animals is difficult to remove

43. Which of the following choices BEST describes the function of the learning curve? It

    A. shows rate of acquisition of a skill
    B. shows how a skill is learned
    C. represents the learning process for acquisition of a skill
    D. represents quantitative and qualitative acquisition of a skill over time

44. Of the following, the psychologist who places LEAST emphasis on practice as a factor in learning is

    A. Thorndike   B. Skinner   C. Hull   D. Guthrie

45. Which one of the following is NOT associated with teaching machines?

    A. Skinner   B. Crowder   C. Pressey   D. Hilgard

46. Which one of the following is NOT a law of perception according to the Gestalt school?

    A. Proximity
    B. Good continuation
    C. Similarity
    D. Readiness

47. Moslow's theory of psychogenic needs in the human organism states that

    A. during the elementary school years, social needs assume more importance than physiological needs
    B. cognitive needs of the child emerge only with considerable stimulation in school
    C. individual differences in strength of needs are so wide that any hierarchy of needs is meaningless
    D. the hierarchy of needs remains constant throughout all of life

48. The neonate is to the infant as the pre-adolescent is to the

    A. primary grade child
    B. early adolescent
    C. middle grade child
    D. young adult

49. A young lady observes that she has lost her wallet. She bursts into tears, sobs loudly, and stamps her foot vigorously. Her behavior is an example of

    A. aggression
    B. projection
    C. resignation
    D. regression

50. A high school boy says to his mother, "I'm doing excellent work in math, history, and biology. However, my teacher is giving me a bare passing grade in Spanish." This comment is an example of

    A. reaction formation
    B. projection
    C. atavism
    D. transference

KEY (CORRECT ANWSWERS)

1. A	11. B	21. B	31. A	41. A
2. D	12. B	22. C	32. B	42. D
3. C	13. A	23. B	33. C	43. A
4. D	14. C	24. D	34. B	44. D
5. C	15. D	25. C	35. C	45. D
6. C	16. B	26. B	36. B	46. D
7. B	17. A	27. C	37. C	47. D
8. D	18. A	28. B	38. D	48. C
9. A	19. C	29. D	39. A	49. D
10. D	20. D	30. B	40. D	50. C

TEST 4

DIRECTIONS: Each question or incomplete statement is followed by several suggested answers or completions. Select the one that *BEST* answers the question or completes the statement. *PRINT THE LETTER OF THE CORRECT ANSWER IN THE SPACE AT THE RIGHT.*

1. According to the norms of the Wechsler-Bellevue Scale, 50% of the general population have I.Q.'s between

    A. 80 and 120
    B. 85 and 115
    C. 90 and 110
    D. 95 and 105

2. Which of the following performance tests of intelligence include a manikin test? The

    A. Arthur Point Scale and the Cornell-Cox, but not the Pintner-Patterson
    B. Arthur Point Scale and the Pintner-Paterson, but not the Cornell-Cox
    C. Cornell-Cox and the Pintner-Paterson, but not the Arthur Point Scale
    D. Arthur Point Scale, the Cornell-Cox, and the Pintner-Paterson

3. How many of the following performance tests of intelligence do *NOT* include a block design test of the Kohs type: the Pintner-Paterson; the Porteus; the Cornell-Cox; the Wechsler-Bellevue Performance Scale?

    A. one B. two C. three D. four

4. Below are two different responses to the "man with umbrella" picture absurdity test I (VII, 1) on the Stanford-Binet,
   Form L (1) "He's going through the rain and he don't know it"
           (2) "He's staying out in the rain"

    A. Both responses are creditable
    B. The first response is creditable but the second response is not
    C. The second response is creditable but the first is not
    D. Neither of the responses is creditable

5. Below are two different responses to the Comprehension III (VII, 4) question on the Stanford-Binet, Form L, "What's the thing for you to do when you have broken something which belongs to someone else?"
    (1) "Be ashamed of yourself"
    (2) "Tell 'em I did it"

    A. Both responses are creditable
    B. The first response is creditable but the second response is not
    C. The second response is creditable but the first is not
    D. Neither of the responses is creditable

6. To receive full credit for the second design (design b) in the Memory for Designs test on the Stanford-Binet, Form L, (IX, 3) the subject must reproduce a design that meets four conditions. Three of the conditions listed are correctly indicated. Which one of the following is INCORRECTLY stated?

    A. The outer figure must be rectangular
    B. The inner rectangle must be in the center

C. The inner figure may appear square but must not be noticeably higher than wide
D. The lines from the corners of the inner rectangles must meet the corners of the outer rectangles fairly accurately

7. Which of the following sentences in the directions for the Stanford-Binet Form L Word Naming test (X, 5) is an unwarranted deviation from the original test instructions?

   A. Now I want to see how many different words you can name in one minute.
   B. Just any words will do—like 'clouds,' 'sky,' 'blue,' 'happy.'
   C. When I say, 'Ready', you begin and say the words as fast as you can and I will count them.
   D. Ready; go ahead.

7._____

8. Which of the following parts of the directions to the Problem Situation test (XI (11)5) of the Stanford-Binet, Form L, represents an unwarranted deviation from the original instructions?

   A. Listen, and see if you can understand what I read.
   B. Donald went walking in the woods. He saw a pretty little animal that he tried to take home for a pet.
   C. It got away from him, but when he got home, his family immediately burned all his clothes.
   D. What was the pretty little animal that he saw?

8._____

9. Below are two different responses to the question as to the difference between *LAZI-NESS* and *IDLENESS* on the Stanford-Binet, Form L (Ave.Adult,3):

   (1) Laziness you just don't want to do anything, while idleness you stop and rest or something like that;
   (2) If you're lazy, you'll do something but you don't like to do it and, if you're idle, you don't do anything.

   A. Both responses are creditable
   B. The first response (1) is creditable, but the second (2) is not
   C. The second response (2) is creditable but the first response (1) is not
   D. Neither of the two responses is creditable

9._____

10. Dementia praecox is a term that was once widely used to describe the condition that is now designated as

    A. melancholia   B. schizophrenia
    C. neurasthenia   D. psychasthenia

10._____

11. When the distinction is made, the idiopathic epilepsies are regarded by writers on the subject as differing from the symptomatic epilepsies in that the former are

    A. manifested in petit mal rather than grand mal attacks
    B. those in which gross lesions cannot be demonstrated
    C. pseudo-epilepsies whose symptoms are of hysterical origin
    D. accompanied by mental deterioration

11._____

12. Which one of the names listed is NOT that of an author of a book on intellectually gifted children?

    A. J.E. Bentley
    B. L.S. Hollingworth
    C. L.M. Terman
    D. F. Tredgold

13. Cretinism is associated with which one of the following types of glandular disfunctioning?

    A. hyperthyroidism
    B. hypothyroidism
    C. hyperpituitarism
    D. hypopituitarism

14. Psychologically, the whole is more than the sum of its parts is a statement which has been quoted most as a tenet of which of the following schools of psychological thought?

    A. Sensationalism
    B. Configurationalism
    C. Psychoanalysis
    D. Structuralism

15. Somatic manifestations of personality disorders are BEST characterized as those which are

    A. hereditary in origin
    B. indicative of structural alteration
    C. revealed in physical functioning
    D. environmentally acquired

16. Of the following characteristics, the one that is MOST common to all types of epilepsy is

    A. recurring lapses of consciousness
    B. mental deterioration
    C. convulsive manifestations
    D. localized brain lesions

17. A child develops a headache every time a particularly distasteful task is announced. This type of reaction is characterized as

    A. hysterical
    B. rationalization
    C. projection
    D. physiological

18. Eidetic images are

    A. subjective visual, auditory, and similar phenomena which assume a perceptual character
    B. pure sensory impressions free of the meaning derived from recognition of objects perceived
    C. hallucinations manifested by adults who, except for this special departure from reality, are normally adjusted
    D. hallucinations manifested by highly suggestible pre-psychotic children

19. In the course of your work as a psychologist you have administered a battery of tests to a boy who is just 12 years old. In intelligence he earned an MA of 14-0. In reading his standard score was 55. In arithmetic his sigma score was +.8. In vocabulary his percentile score was 78. If all boys of his age were ranked according to their scores on each of these four tests, this boy's standing would be highest in

    A. intelligence
    B. reading
    C. arithmetic
    D. vocabulary

Questions 20-24.

Questions 20 to 24 are based on the following table representing the frequency with which children of various ages between 7 and 13 expressed their preference for certain occupations, designated respectively M, N, O and P. Each child was asked to indicate which of the four occupations he would like best to enter. Age at last birthday is shown in the left hand column of the table; the four remaining columns give the frequency with which children in each age group chose the respective occupations whose code letters M, N, O or P are indicated at the top.

NOTE: The questions have been framed in such a way as to enable the candidate to answer them by inspection of the data without the necessity of making the actual computations.

OCCUPATIONAL CHOICES OF CHILDREN OF VARIOUS AGES

AGE	M	N	O	P	Total
13	1	10	5	2	18
12	2	11	2	2	19
11	2	6	4	6	18
10	3	3	2	9	17
9	5	5	3	7	20
8	7	3	4	3	17
7	4	2	2	1	9
Total	24	40	22	32	118

20. For which occupation is the MEAN age of children choosing that occupation highest? 20.____

    A. Occupation M   B. Occupation N
    C. Occupation O   D. Occupation P

21. For which occupation is the MEDIAN age of the children choosing that occupation lowest? 21.____

    A. M   B. N   C. O   D. P

22. In which distribution is the average deviation greatest? 22.____

    A. M   B. N   C. O   D. P

23. In which distribution is the age equivalent of the 75th percentile highest? 23.____

    A. M   B. N   C. O   D. P

24. If you wished to compute the relationship between age and choice of occupation, which one of the following coefficients of correlations could you compute from the data? 24.____

    A. Pearson Product-Moment r
    B. Bi-serial r
    C. Spearman rho
    D. Correlation ratio eta

Questions 25-30.

Questions 25 to 30 are based on the following case description:

Grace is referred to psychological study because her work is poor, she has unexplained absences from school, she whispers very often, and sometimes talks back to the teacher. She is 12 years, 2 months old and is in a 6B class. Her I.Q. on the Revised Stanford-Binet, Form L, is 84. Achievement grade scores are: Reading Comprehension, 4.2; Vocabulary 4.8; Spelling 5.5; Arithmetic reasoning 4.6; Arithmetic Computation 3.7. Her work has always been poor, but until this year she always behaved well in school. Her mother complains of a similar change from obedience to disobedience at home.

25. For a more careful diagnosis of Grace's difficulties in computation, the psychologist may choose to employ the Buswell-John Diagnostic Charts because they

    A. have carefully standardized norms for each operation
    B. have the examples arranged by grade levels
    C. help one to discover quickly which number combinations the child does not know
    D. provide a method for acting and recording all the steps in the solution of each example

26. During an interview, Grace complains that her present teacher is nasty and sarcastic. The girl says that she behaves poorly in school because of the teacher. Grace's explanation

    A. is an example of projection and indicates a paranoid trend
    B. is probably correct since teachers are much too prone to use sarcasm
    C. may be partially true but does not explain her behavior at home
    D. reveals the futility of seeking factual information by interviewing pupils

27. If Grace's I.Q. remains constant, her mental age (on the Stanford-Binet) at maturity will be about

    A. 11 years 9 months   B. 12 years 6 months
    C. 13 years 3 months   D. 14 years 0 months

28. In describing Grace's mental ability in a report, the psychologist would be most accurate in calling her

    A. borderline   B. dull normal
    C. high-grade defective   D. low average

29. It is a reasonable expectation that Grace will

    A. be graduated from a vocational high school course
    B. fail to be promoted beyond the seventh grade
    C. fail to reach the median standards of the tenth grade
    D. leave school at the age of 14

30. In view of her age and intelligence, Grace's achievement in reading is

    A. about one year better than such girls usually achieve
    B. at just about normal expectancy
    C. mainly responsible for her poor work in other school subjects
    D. sufficiently poor to be called a disability

Questions 31-41.

Questions 31 to 41 are based on the following case description:

Martin is referred for psychological examination because at the age of 11-6 he is still a total non-reader. His I.Q. is found to be 86. The psychologist notes that in performance tests he does much better with tests involving pictures than in block-design tests, and that in taking the Rorschach he begins on each card by listing the colors on it.

31. On the basis of these two indications, the psychologist should look carefully for further evidence of

    A. neurotic instability
    B. organic brain defect
    C. psychopathic impulsiveness
    D. schizoid trends

32. A medical examination indicates that Martin is a case of Frohlich's syndrome. For further study and treatment of this condition, he should be referred to

    A. an endocrinologist
    B. an otorhynologist
    C. an orthopaedic specialist
    D. a psychiatrist

33. To check the adequacy of Martin's efficiency in binocular vision, which of the following instruments could be used best?

    A. a Flashmeter
    B. a Metron-O-Scope
    C. a Telebinocular
    D. a Visuoscope

34. The psychologist finds that Martin used to be left-handed but is now right-handed. If the psychologist accepts Orton's theory, he will conclude that

    A. emotional disturbance was created by the way in which Martin was forced to use his right hand
    B. there is a conflict between a natural tendency to move from right to left and an imposed pattern of movement from left to right
    C. there is confusion between memory traces in Martin's left and right cerebral hemispheres
    D. there is no causal relationship between Martin's handedness and his reading disability

35. A series of diagnostic reading tests that could be used profitably by the psychologist examining Martin was devised by

    A. G.L. Buswell
    B. M. Monroe
    C. S.L. Pressey
    D. L.L. Thurstone

36. After further study, the psychologist decides to recommend the use of the Fernald method of teaching non-readers.
    This method places great emphasis upon

    A. developing visual memory through tachistoscopic presentation of digits, letters and words
    B. learning letter sounds and how to blend them
    C. tracing words and then writing them from memory
    D. using workbooks in which words are associated with pictures

37. If Fernald's procedure is followed, the reading material used in the early stages of remedial work will be

    A. reading readiness workbooks
    B. special remedial workbooks
    C. stories dictated by Martin
    D. typical first grade readers and workbooks

38. If, on the other hand, the psychologist decided to follow the general procedure recommended by Gates, he would emphasize

    A. learning a short selection by heart and then looking at the words while reciting the story
    B. systematic letter-by-letter phonics
    C. tracing words and then writing them from memory
    D. visual word study with supplementary word analysis

39. The most practical method of coming to a tentative choice of method to be followed in the early stages of remedial work with Martin is to

    A. compare his results on tests of visual memory, auditory memory, and motor control
    B. find out what method was used by his first grade teacher and choose a method as different as possible
    C. give him brief sample lessons with several different methods
    D. recommend the use of the method with which the prospective tutor is most experienced

40. Martin's mother asks what she should do about his reading at home. In situations like this the mother should usually be advised to

    A. deprive him of privileges if he doesn't do his assigned work
    B. have Martin read to her so that she can correct his errors
    C. leave the remedial work entirely in the hands of the tutor
    D. review the whole of each lesson with him when he gets home

41. Martin is now in a 4B class, having repeated four terms, is well liked by the teacher and never misbehaves. The principal wants to know what to do with him at the end of the term. Assuming that private remedial lessons are to be given outside of school hours, the principal should be advised to

    A. have him repeat the 4B grade
    B. place him in a C.R.M.D. class
    C. place Martin in an Op ABCD class
    D. promote him to a slow 5A class

Questions 42-43.

Questions 42 and 43 are based on the following case description:

Joseph is 14 years 6 months old and in a regular 7B class in junior high school. His teachers complain that he is inattentive and uninterested. He has six unexplained absences this term. Psychometric findings are: Wechsler-Bellevue Total I.Q. 92, Verbal I.Q. 84, Performance I.Q. 97, reading comprehension 6.2, arithmetic computation 6.6, mechanical assembly test 40th percentile for his age.

42. For exploration of Joseph's vocational interests, the psychologist should rely primarily on   42._____

    A. an interview
    B. the Cleeton Vocational Interest Inventory
    C. the Kuder Preference Record
    D. the Strong Vocational Interest Blank

43. It develops that Joseph is treated very badly at home by his stepmother, who resents his   43._____
    close resemblance to his mother. His father beats him severely, sometimes without
    cause. Of the following recommendations the best one would probably be to recommend

    A. consideration of foster home placement
    B. placement in a state school because of his truancy
    C. that the parents be advised that they will have to treat him better or be taken to
       court
    D. a Big Brother contact

Questions 44 to 48 are based on the following case description:

Richard was referred for study because he was considered to be restless, inattentive, talkative, and a disturbing influence in the classroom. Psychometric data are as follows: present grade 5.2, C.A. 10-8, Stanford-Binet, Form L., M.A. 14-6, I.Q. 140, achievement grade levels – Reading comprehension 8.7, Spelling 7.9, Arithmetic Computation 7.6, Arithmetic Reasoning 8.8.

44. Assuming continued normal development, it is MOST probable that he   44._____

    A. will be a very superior student in high school and a superior student in college
    B. will be a superior student in high school and an average student in college
    C. should be considered a potential genius
    D. will be more successful as an engineer or scientist than as a lawyer or physician

45. Of the following tentative hypotheses, the one which is the MOST probable explanation   45._____
    of his classroom behavior is that he

    A. has been badly spoiled at home
    B. suffers from hyperthyroidism
    C. is a case of primary behavior disorder
    D. is not sufficiently challenged by the classroom work

46. The psychologist is probably justified in recommending to Richard's present teacher that   46._____

    A. he appoint a committee of three pupils to recommend to the class how they should
       treat Richard
    B. his conduct should be accepted without adverse comment
    C. Richard should assist the teacher by reporting instances of misbehavior by other
       members of the class
    D. Richard should be permitted to assume special study assignments

47. Richard's mother complains that none of his teachers has understood or appreciated him. She says he is a model child at home and refuses to believe that he misbehaves in school. The psychologist is justified in

    A. accepting her statements at face value
    B. suspecting that Richard is overindulged at home
    C. encouraging her to place him in a private school where he will be appreciated
    D. telling her that she has been guilty of spoiling him very badly

48. The average Accomplishment Quotient for children with I.Q.'s of 120 or more has been found to be

    A. below 100
    B. at 100
    C. approximately 110
    D. at 120 or above

Questions 49-50.

Questions 49 to 50 are based on the following case description:

Cynthia, a 10-year-old girl of normal intelligence and scholarship is reported by her mother to talk in her sleep, to walk in her sleep occasionally, to have intense crying spells on little provocation, and to have a violent temper when she does not get her own way.

49. The psychologist's tentative diagnosis would be that Cynthia is showing signs of

    A. hysteria
    B. psychopathic personality
    C. dementia praecox
    D. psychasthenia

50. A psychiatrist would probably be most interested in getting from the psychologist, in addition to findings about mental ability and scholastic achievement, an analysis of Cynthia's

    A. dreams, wishes and fears
    B. attitudes toward her parents and siblings
    C. vocational ambitions and interests
    D. responses in projective tests

KEY (CORRECT ANSWERS)

1. C	11. B	21. A	31. B	41. D
2. D	12. D	22. C	32. A	42. A
3. B	13. B	23. B	33. C	43. A
4. B	14. B	24. D	34. C	44. A
5. D	15. C	25. C	35. B	45. D
6. B	16. A	26. C	36. C	46. D
7. B	17. A	27. B	37. C	47. B
8. D	18. A	28. B	38. D	48. A
9. A	19. A	29. C	39. C	49. A
10. B	20. B	30. B	40. C	50. D

TEST 5

DIRECTIONS: Each question or incomplete statement is followed by several suggested answers or completions. Select the one that BEST answers the question or completes the statement. PRINT THE LETTER OF THE CORRECT ANSWER IN THE SPACE AT THE RIGHT.

Questions 1-6.
Questions 1 to 6 deal with an eleven-year-old boy who is referred to a child guidance clinic by his teacher as a behavior problem.

1. As a supplement to the psychological examination, the psychologist will probably get most light on the child's problem by

   A. examining samples of his school work
   B. filling out a behavior rating scale
   C. observing him in the classroom
   D. using a personality inventory

2. In planning a test battery for the child, which of the following would be most suitable in establishing learning potentiality?

   A. The Stanford-Binet
   B. The Pintner-Patterson
   C. The Wechsler-Bellevue
   D. The Kuhlmann-Anderson

3. Under the State Mental Hygiene Law, this boy could not be classified as mentally defective if his I.Q. were above

   A. 50   B. 60   C. 65   D. 75

4. When you examine his school record card you learn that he had previously been given a National Intelligence Test, on which he received a low score, and a Pintner-Cunningham Test, on which he received a high score. The discrepancy between the two scores suggests the likelihood of

   A. an auditory defect
   B. emotional instability
   C. a motor handicap
   D. reading disability

5. After you have examined the boy and found that he has an I.Q. of 65 and that placement in a class for retarded children is indicated, the boy's parents protest your recommendation. In an interview with the mother directed to getting her to accept your recommendation, the emphasis should be on

   A. explaining the provisions of the state law
   B. indicating that such placement is only temporary
   C. demonstrating the extent of the child's handicap
   D. pointing to the advantages to the child of special class placement

6. On the basis of all the evidence you have examined, you form the tentative hypothesis that this boy's difficulties grow out of his "rejection" by his mother. In interpreting this child's difficulties in an interview with his mother, it is well to begin by

   A. letting her know how much you like the child
   B. listening sympathetically as she recounts her difficulties in dealing with him
   C. making it clear that her attitude is responsible for his problem
   D. stressing the child's assets

Questions 7-10.

Questions 7 to 10 are based on the following situation:

Theresa M. is the unhappy child of an unhappy marriage. The mother is an embittered and disillusioned woman who is determined that her daughter shall never make the same mistake of marrying the wrong man. Theresa is, therefore, required to come home immediately after she is dismissed from the high school she attends. The girl is never permitted to participate in extra-curricular activities after school hours or to attend parties at other classmates' homes. The father, a solemn hardworking man, supports the family adequately but has given up all attempts at getting along with his wife. At home, he is quiet and uncommunicative. After he has eaten his evening meal, he either reads his newspaper until bed-time or goes to a neighborhood grill for a few glasses of beer and an evening of talk with friends.

7. According to current psychological opinion if Theresa had not been referred to the clinic, by the age of 20 she probably would have

    A. become psychotic
    B. outgrown her asocial traits
    C. run away from home
    D. remained a shy, asocial person

8. When the girl, a timid, asocial adolescent, is referred to the clinic by the principal of the school she attends, the primary responsibility of the clinic is to try to

    A. uncover the conscious and unconscious motivation for the mother's attitude
    B. get the father to play a more aggressive role in the family
    C. improve the girl's emotional adjustment
    D. effect a reconciliation between the parents

9. The principal has suggested that Theresa be placed in a foster home. This proposal is

    A. a practicable one if funds are available to pay for her board
    B. a practicable one if test results indicate that she will stay in high school long enough to get a diploma
    C. an impracticable one since the parents will probably not agree to the arrangement
    D. an impracticable one since adolescents are too old for placement in a foster home

10. The mother's attitude can BEST be categorized as

    A. regression
    B. projection
    C. negativism
    D. psychotic

Questions 11-17.

Questions 11 to 17 are based on the following case description:

Allen is referred for psychological examination soon after he enters a public school at the age of seven. He is a short, overweight boy with a brachycephalic head, large fissured tongue, very short fingers, the little finger uncurved, and definite epicanthic folds. On the Revised Stanford-Binet, Form L, his M.A. is 3 years 2 months and his I.Q. is 45.

11. In expressing the degree of Allen's mental retardation, the psychologist would be most justified in describing him as

   A. a low grade moron
   B. a high grade imbecile
   C. a low grade imbecile
   D. an idiot

12. Judging from the data given, Allen seems to be a case of which clinical type of mental deficiency?

   A. Mongolism
   B. Cretinism
   C. Brachycephalism
   D. Dystrophism

13. In the City, such children as Allen are usually recommended for placement in

   A. a regular CRMD class
   B. a low I.Q.
   C. a vestibule class
   D. an Op ABCD class

14. Although not conclusively proved, an explanation of Allen's condition that has been widely propounded is associated with

   A. an inherited condition of recessive type
   B. malnutrition during the prenatal development
   C. reproductive exhaustion in the mother
   D. injury during birth

15. The outlook for Allen's future is that he will be, when adult,

   A. capable of doing semi-skilled labor
   B. partially self-supporting at unskilled labor
   C. unemployable but capable of self-care in a protected environment
   D. almost completely helpless

16. If intensive medical treatment had been given to him in early childhood, one might have expected

   A. no marked improvement from any kind of medical treatment now available
   B. substantial improvement from thyroid therapy
   C. substantial improvement from polyglandular therapy
   D. substantial improvement from a high-vitamin, mineral-rich diet

17. Allen's mother is worried over the fact that he still wets the bed almost every night. The psychologist should explain to her that

   A. this demonstrates that something in the way he is treated at home has made him nervous
   B. he probably has weak kidneys for which he should have ample liquid intake
   C. she has not been consistent enough in training him
   D. this may be part of his general slowness in growing

Questions 18-21.

Questions 18 to 21 are based on the following situation:

In response to the principal's request, you have been assigned the task of helping the pupils who are about to be graduated from the junior high school to choose their high schools wisely. The following problems arise from this assignment:

18. You are called upon to interview the over-anxious mother of one of the boys whom you have tested. You think that one aspect of his problem is the fact that the mother's academic ambitions for him are too high. She is set on a professional career for him even though he has an I.Q. of 95. Your interview may well begin by

    A. encouraging her to talk about other phases of his adjustment in which he has been successful
    B. indicating that eventually he may achieve all she expects of him
    C. making it clear that in all probability he will not be able to complete an academic high school course
    D. showing her how her attitude has aggravated his problem

18.____

19. A girl who contemplates taking a specialized visual arts course in high school asks for aptitude tests. A test which may be used as a basis for discussing her plans is the one devised by

    A. Seashore
    B. McAdory
    C. Macquarrie
    D. Stenquist

19.____

20. On the preliminary questionnaire distributed by the principal to all members of the graduating class, a fifteen-year-old boy indicated that he would like to have your advice on the choice of a high school. As the first step, you should

    A. administer intelligence and aptitude tests
    B. give an interest inventory
    C. consult the boy's school record card
    D. interview the boy

20.____

21. George L., one of the boys in this group, is interested in learning how to play the piano. His father asks you for an estimate of the boy's talent in music in order to decide whether or not to pay for these lessons. To help you to arrive at a decision, which of the following tests would you administer?

    A. Ishi-Hara
    B. Kwalwasser-Dykema
    C. Minnesota
    D. Monroe

21.____

Questions 22-33.

Questions 22 to 33 are based on the following situation:

After a city-wide survey, the test results in a certain school are so unusual that you, a school psychologist, are assigned to the school in order to interpret the results to the principal and teachers, to administer such additional tests as you think necessary, and to attempt to discover the reasons for the atypical results in this school.

22. A number of the seventh grade pupils obtained I.Q.'s under 75 on the Pintner-General Abilities, Verbal Series. Upon checking their reading grades, you find that these children are poor readers. These findings indicate that

   A. these pupils are not likely to profit from a remedial reading program since their intelligence is so low
   B. these children are eligible for placement in C.R.M.D. classes
   C. the test may not be valid for these children
   D. the children are, in fact, not truly retarded in intelligence

23. On the California Mental Maturity Scale, a child obtained an I.Q. of 85 on the language section and an I.Q. of 45 on the non-language section. Of the following explanations, the one which is MOST probable is that the child

   A. has an exceptionally good vocabulary
   B. has an organic defect
   C. is primarily intellectual in his interests
   D. lacks common sense

24. The Metropolitan Intermediate Achievement Battery (designed for grades 4, 5, and 6) has been administered to a sixth grade class. Of the following, the soundest basis for selecting children for a remedial program in reading is a comparison of their reading level with expectancy based on their

   A. achievement in other school subjects
   B. chronological age
   C. grade placement
   D. mental age

25. The children in the first half of the second grade were given a reading test designed for use in second and third grades. The test scores are MOST accurate for the group consisting of the

   A. best readers B. brightest children
   C. dullest children D. poorest readers

26. A group of children ranging in age from seven to twelve years of age arrived recently at this school. The principal asks you to recommend a test of which he can administer a single form to this entire group at one time and that will lead to an approximation of their computational skill. For this purpose he should use the

   A. Metropolitan B. Progressive
   C. Stanford D. Woody-McCall

27. The MOST effective use you could make of behavior rating scales is to employ them in

   A. getting teachers to analyze their impressions of children
   B. making reports to parents
   C. demonstrating to children the nature of their shortcomings
   D. understanding the dynamics of behavior

28. It would be justifiable to use personality schedules in order to 28.____

    A. diagnose neuroses
    B. make pupils aware of their problems
    C. survey a group in order to select extreme cases for further study
    D. understand family relationships in their effect on child behavior

29. A six-year-old is referred to you by the principal for assistance in correct class placement. 29.____
    The youngster's Stanford-Binet I.Q. is 85. Which of the following would you use as a supplementary test?

    A. Arthur   B. Merrill-Palmer
    C. Kuhlmann-Binet   D. Wechsler-Bellevue

30. A twelve-year-old boy has just arrived from the South where he had only one year of 30.____
    schooling. Under these circumstances, which of the following test scores would you regard as being MOST nearly representative of his potential?

    A. Reading Grade 3.5
    B. Stanford-Binet Form L I.Q. 70
    C. Wechsler-Bellevue Performance I.Q. 95
    D. Wechsler-Bellevue Verbal I.Q. 65

31. The principal tells you of a mother who visited him that morning to request that her 5 1/2- 31.____
    year-old daughter be transferred from the kindergarten to the first grade. On a recent psychological examination the youngster had a Stanford-Binet I.Q. of 130. As a basis for decision, which of the following would be MOST helpful?

    A. Estimate of social maturity
    B. Merrill-Palmer
    C. Pintner-Cunningham
    D. Thematic Apperception

32. You plan to administer to the entire school a group intelligence test with which you have 32.____
    had a great deal of experience over a period of years. It is your considered opinion that the test is a very good one but that too much time is allotted to one part of the test. Your decision concerning the desirability of adjusting the timing of the test for this school should be based on the principle that

    A. directions for administering tests are intended for the guidance of imperfectly trained examiners and may be discarded by experienced examiners
    B. good clinical judgment is preferable to literal interpretation of directions for administering tests
    C. strict adherence to the directions contained in the test manual are important only when one is engaged in research
    D. the time allotments indicated in the test manual should be followed even though the examiner thinks the timing is improper

33. The teachers in this school are cooperative and eager to assist you in the testing pro- 33.____
    gram. You know little, however, of their technical competence beyond that to be expected from a group of experienced teachers. If you had only a one hour teacher's meeting in which to explain suitable procedures to be followed, you should use their services in

A. administering standardized group tests
B. giving individual performance tests
C. interpreting test results for individual guidance
D. selecting tests to be administered to various pupils

Questions 34-39.

Questions 34 to 39 deal with the construction of the test described below:
A test is being constructed in order to indicate which elementary school graduates can use verbal symbols sufficiently well to warrant their undertaking the study of a foreign language in high school with a good chance of completing the course successfully.

34. For such a test, the BEST single kind of validation is to

A. make an item analysis using total test scores as the criterion
B. pool the opinion of progressive language teachers
C. correlate the test scores with standardized achievement test scores earned as the result of instruction in high school language courses
D. compare the newly constructed test with other published measures of language aptitude appropriate for use with similar pupils

35. It is preferable to have multiple choice items rather than completion items on this test because

A. completion scores cannot be corrected for guessing
B. completion items usually prove to be too difficult for the pupils
C. it is more difficult to score completion items objectively
D. pupils are more familiar with multiple choice tests

36. After some months of preliminary research you have a form of the test ready for trial administration. In order to evaluate the validity and reliability of this test, it should be tried out on a group consisting of

A. good students
B. poor students
C. students of average ability
D. students of varied ability

37. One of the large city high schools cooperating in this test construction project permits all entering students to study a foreign language if they so wish. If a student is failing in this subject at the end of his first two months in high school, he is dropped from the class and the notation "Dropped-below 65%" is entered on his record as his final mark in that subject. The remaining members of the class continue until the end of the term and receive a per cent mark. About a fifth of each entering class are dropped from the course at the end of the first term.
If you wish to find the central tendency of the final marks in language for the entire freshman class, the MOST appropriate measure to use is the

A. median   B. mode
C. harmonic mean   D. arithmetic mean

38. One of the language teachers who is assisting in the construction of this test expresses the hope that the test will be so good that, when the raw scores are transmuted into standard scores, a standard score of 80 will indicate the presence of twice as much of the tested ability as is indicated by a standard score of 40.

    This teacher's hope

    A. will probably not be realized because of the absence of a true zero in this type of mental measurement
    B. will probably not be realized because of the difficulty of making the test sufficiently reliable
    C. will be realized provided that the test is adequately validated
    D. may be realized only if there is a symmetrical distribution of language potentiality in the group tested

39. When you correlate the results of this test with the scores on a nationally known test of foreign language aptitude, you are amazed to discover that r = .98.

    You are justified in concluding that

    A. you should continue this test construction project since your test is a good one
    B. your test must contain some of the items from the published test
    C. language competence is so complex that more than one test in this area is needed
    D. this test is not likely to yield much greater accuracy of prediction than does the published test

40. Marie, 15 years old, is referred by the counselor in her high school because her work has declined from an 85 percent average last year to failing in three subjects. During examination she seems vague, listless, and apathetic. Her verbal I.Q. is 115 and her performance I.Q. is 95 with marked unevenness of functioning, failing easy items and passing harder ones. Her mother reports that Marie has no friends and spends most of her spare time in her own room. The psychologist should first

    A. attempt to complete a differential diagnosis
    B. refer Marie for psychiatric study
    C. make a careful study of her vocational aptitudes and interests
    D. request a thorough medical examination

41. A contemporary book by Albert Deutsch is of interest to psychologists because it is concerned with

    A. a history of the treatment of the mentally ill
    B. conditions in state hospitals
    C. treatment in state prisons
    D. juvenile delinquency and institutions for delinquents

Questions 42-50.

Questions 42 to 50 are based upon the following case description:

Peter, a ten-year-old, is reported for failure to show adequate progress in school work. He has his teacher perplexed because he does superior art work and construction, seems to work well when she works alone with him but seems to be in a fog most of the time. He never seems to pay attention in the group. Directions have to be repeated over and over, and then he will ask, "What?" His mother says he is the same at home, never does anything when he is first asked, complies only when she loses patience and shouts at him. His teacher wonders at times whether he is a proper candidate for a class for children with retarded mental development or whether he is living in a dream world. He seems well accepted by the other children, is often chosen by them, and gets along well with them in play.

During the Binet examination the psychologist noted that on a few occasions, Peter misunderstood a question because he confused a word with a similar sounding one. In his own conversation and in his responses he did not show such substitutions. He did especially well copying designs and on all visual test items. His cooperation was good and he seemed thoroughly interested in the examination tasks. His ratings on the Arthur scale were consistently high. The I.Q. obtained on the Arthur was 115, on the Binet 106.

He enjoyed the Rorschach, responded rapidly and freely with 30 responses, 2M, 2FM, 7P, 4 FC, 2 CF, and OC.

42. On the basis of the available evidence which one of the following is most needed in starting the further examination of this case?

    A. Audiometer
    B. Electroencephalogram
    C. Telebinocular
    D. Sociogram

42.___

43. On the basis of the examination results, the most accurate description of his intellectual ability at this time is

    A. average
    B. superior
    C. at least average, probably higher
    D. at least superior, probably very superior

43.___

44. To be eligible for C.R.M.D. class placement Peter's I.Q. on the Binet would have to be

    A. between 50 and 70
    B. between 50 and 75
    C. between 30 and 70
    D. between 30 and 85

44.___

45. In determining eligibility for C.R.M.D. class placement, mental age

    A. is not considered apart from IQ
    B. must be between 5 years 0 months and 8 years 0 months
    C. must be at least 5 years 0 months
    D. must be under 8 years 0 months

45.___

46. What is reported about Peter's performance on the Arthur Scale

    A. makes one suspect emotional insecurity
    B. need not indicate psychopathology
    C. indicates superior mechanical aptitude
    D. makes one suspect an organic brain lesion

46.___

47. On the basis of the Rorschach results, which one of the following characteristics is most accurate in describing Peter?   47.____

    A. Withdrawn
    C. Outgoing
    B. Constricted
    D. Egocentric

48. The experience balance on the Rorschach, as it would be computed by Klopfer, is in this case   48.____

    A. 4:6   B. 2:4   C. 4:4   D. 2:6

49. On the basis of the Rorschach, which one of the following is the most accurate description of Peter's affect?   49.____

    A. Flat
    C. Uncontrolled
    B. Repressed
    D. Well balanced

50. If we assume that the rest of the Rorschach confirms the findings already given, present results indicate   50.____

    A. emotional instability
    B. neurotic disturbance
    C. possible organic brain lesion
    D. no pathology

KEY (CORRECT ANSWERS)

1. C	11. B	21. B	31. A	41. D
2. A	12. A	22. C	32. D	42. A
3. D	13. B	23. B	33. A	43. C
4. D	14. C	24. D	34. C	44. B
5. D	15. C	25. A	35. C	45. C
6. B	16. A	26. D	36. D	46. B
7. D	17. D	27. A	37. A	47. C
8. C	18. A	28. C	38. A	48. B
9. C	19. B	29. B	39. D	49. D
10. B	20. C	30. C	40. B	50. D

Glossary of Psychometric Terms

TABLE OF CONTENTS

	Page
Ability Tests ... Bimodal	1
Central Tendency ... Correlation	2
Criterion ... Distribution	3
Equivalent Form ... Frequency Distribution	4
Grade Equivalent ... Interval Scale	5
Level of Significance ... Nominal Scale	6
Normal Curve ... Practice Effect	7
Pretest ... Ranking	8
Rating ... Scaling	9
Scaling ... Statistical Procedures	10
Statistic(s) ... Variance	11

Glossary (of Psychometric Terms)

ABILITY TESTS
Tests that purport to measure an individual's over-all facility in doing given things. Often a distinction is attempted between that facility which results from heredity and that which results from learning. In such cases, *ability* tests are usually applied to the "native" aspect and *achievement* tests to the learned aspect.
E-IQ tests, Dominance test.

ACHIEVEMENT TESTS
Tests that purport to measure an individual performance or competence relative to a given subject, usually a subject taught in the schools. Achievement tests are concerned with learned outcomes (generally knowledge and/or understanding) rather than "native" capacity or ability to learn the subject.
EX-Metropolitan Achievement Tests, MacGinitie.

AGE EQUIVALENTS
A method of expressing scores on standardized tests. The raw score typical of pupils of different ages is determined and then any pupil's raw score may be converted to the age to which it pertains. Usually given in years and months.
EX-Mental age = 12.6; reading age = 10.4.

APPLIED RESEARCH
Aims to solve an immediate practical problem. It is research performed in relation to actual problems and under conditions in which they are found in practice.
EX-Is *oral presentation or written presentation* more effective in *improving students' performance on tests? Is reading comprehension improved* by using the *individualized approach* as opposed to the *traditional reading group approach?*

BAR GRAPH
Any graphic presentation that uses bars of various length to symbolize differences in quantity, size, amount, etc.

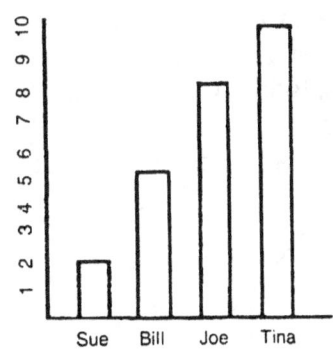

BASIC RESEARCH
Has as its aim obtaining data that can be used to formulate, expand, or evaluate theory. Its essential aim is to expand the frontiers of knowledge without regard to practical application, though the results may be used to solve practical problems.
EX-Is there a relationship between disruptive behavior and reading achievement? Is there a relationship between oral language skills and written language skills?

BIMODAL
A distribution of measures, particularly test scores, with two foci of central tendency rather than one. A superficial indication of bimoesdality is the presence of two modes separated by scores or score intervals whose frequency is appreciably less than that of the modes. Bimodality in a distribution can be suggestive of several attributes of the group or of the test or other measuring procedure in use. It often indicates that the group which is bimodal involves two subgroups having important mean differences as to age, mentality, reading ability, nationality, etc.
Ex-

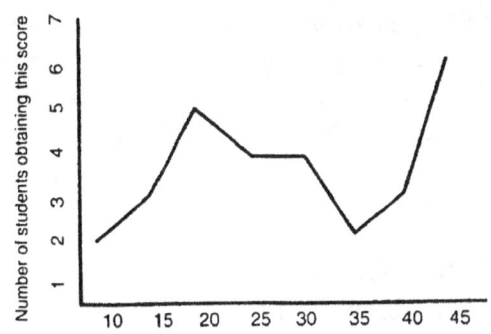

125

CENTRAL TENDENCY
In a distribution of scores or other measures, the point or interval at which a plurality or majority of scores tends to cluster. Unless there is such a clustering, the distribution has no central tendency.
EX-All distributions have a central tendency

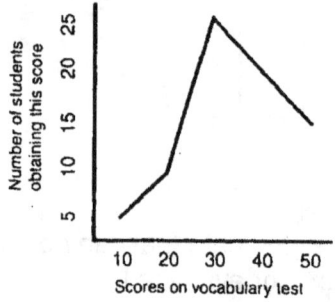

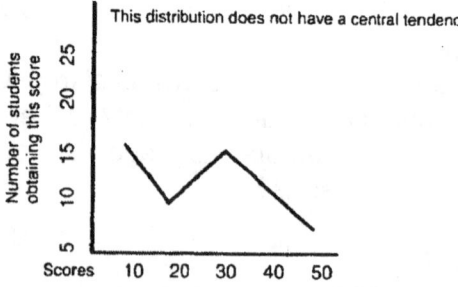

This distribution does not have a central tendency

CHECK LISTS
A device used in observation to direct attention to factors to be observed and sometimes to provide space for recording ratings or comments relative to them.
EX-
1. Can read accurately at a rate of 15 words/minute.
2. Can discriminate between two similarly spelled words.
3. Can follow orally given direction.

C.A. (CHRONOLOGICAL AGE)
A child's age expressed in years and months. Used in reckoning the intelligence quotient and any other index involving a comparison between skill or knowledge and age.
EX-Billy is five years and three months old. His C.A. = 5.3.

CLASSIFICATION
One of four basic forms of measurement (types of measurement symbols). Involves the establishment of categories (classification), the designation of symbols for the categories, and then the assignment of the symbols to phenomena according to the category to which they belong. This is sometimes referred to as the Nominal Level of measurement.
EX-Blood typing, draft classifications; A, B, C, D, F, as course marks.

COEFFICIENT OF CORRELATION (r)
A measure of the degree with which the variation of one variable
is associated with variation of another variable.
EX-

	Intelligence	Grades	Conclusion
Joe	118 (2)	3.5 gpa	
Sue	103 (4)	2.5 gpa	If you have high in
Fred	110 (3)	2.0 gpa	telligence you'll
Linda	130 (1)	4.0 gpa	have high grades

CONCEPT
An abstraction from observed events; it is a word that represents the similarities or common aspects of objects or events that are otherwise quite different from one another. The purpose of a concept is to simplify thinking by including a number of events under one general heading.
EX-Words such as chair, dog, tree, liquor and thousands of others in our language represent common aspects of otherwise diverse things.

CONSTRUCTS
Higher level abstractions that cannot be easily illustrated by pointing to specific objects or events.
EX-Problem-solving ability, motivation, justice or intelligence.

CORRELATION
The statistical technique used for measuring the degree of relationship between two variables is called *correlation*. Correlation shows us the extent to which values in one variable are linked or related to values in another variable. An important use of such measurement is in prediction. When correlational analysis indicates some degree of relationship between two variables, we can use the information

about one of them to make predictions about the other. EX-Having found that intelligence and achievement are correlated, one can make predictions about the future achievement of school children from the results of a test of intelligence given at the beginning of the school year. The accuracy of such prediction is a function of the degree of relationship; that is, the extent of the correlation. The higher the correlation, the more accurate the predictions.

CRITERION
Anything with which a measuring procedure is compared in determining its validity. Specifically a measuring procedure for a given phenomenon for which exemplary validity is claimed or assumed and with which other similar procedures are asked to have high positive correlations.
EX-To show your reading program's effectiveness, you decide all children must advance one year in ability to read. The improvement goal of one year is your criterion.

CUMULATIVE FREQUENCY
A column in a conventional tabulation of scores or other measures that shows the frequency of scores up to and including any given interval.
EX-

No. of students receiving score	Score	Cumulative frequency
1	98	9
2	95	8
3	80	6
2	78	3
1	75	1

DERVIED SCORE
A test score that has been converted to an index of rank, scale position, or classification, as distinct from a raw score, which is the number of correct responses or the immediate numerical weight given the test. Percentile rank, standard scores, mental age.
EX-A child gets 9 spelling words right out of 10; he got a 90%. He did better than all the rest of the class. His derived score is A.

DEPENDENT VARIABLES
Variables that are a consequence of or dependent upon antecedent variables. In research studies, the dependent variable is the phenomenon that is the object of study and investigation. It is the one that must always be assessed.
EX-This is sometimes called assigned variable.

DESCRIPTION
An informal type of measurement expression used to indicate the status of phenomena in which ordinary language is used. The information is not quantified. This is also called the Nominal level of measurement.
EX-Scale rank and classification symbols associated with appraisal of citizenship, study habits, social adjustment.

DESCRIPTIVE RESEARCH
Describes and interprets *what is*. It is concerned with conditions or relationships that exist; practices that prevail; beliefs, points of view, or attitudes that are held; processes that are going on; effects that are being felt; or trends that are developing.
EX-There are several subcategories of descriptive research:
a. Case studies
b. Surveys
c. Developmental studies
d. Follow-up studies
e. Documentary analysis
f. Trend studies
g. Correlational studies

DEVIATION
Departure from a given condition. In particular, the numerical difference between a test score or other measure of an individual and given point of reference, usually the mean of a group of test scores or other measures.
EX-The class average on a test = 85, Jill received a 35. This is a large deviation.

DISTRIBUTION
A table or graph showing the scores or other measures found for a group, so arranged that the number who have a given score or who fall within a given range of scores is apparent.
EX-

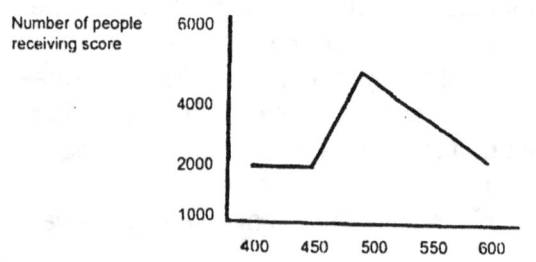

EQUIVALENT FORM
Either of two forms of a measuring instrument, particularly a standardized test which is parallel in content, difficulty, and norms, but different as to terms.
EX-Stanford-Binet Forms L and M.

EVALUATION
The process of assigning symbols to phenomena. These symbols
signify the worth of the phenomena relative to some scheme of
value.
EX-Grading student's paragraphs A, B, C, D or F.

EXPERIMENTAL DESIGN
The conceptual framework within which the experiment is conducted. It serves two functions. It provides opportunity for the comparisons required by the hypotheses of the experiment and it enables the experimenter through his statistical analysis of the data to make a meaningful interpretation of the results of the study.
EX-
  One group → pretest → treatment → post-test
  Exp.group → pretest → treatment I → post-test
  Control group → treatment II

EXPERIMENTAL RESEARCH
A scientific investigation in which an investigator manipulates and controls one or more independent variables and observes the dependent variable or variables for variation concomitant to the manipulation of the independent variables. Its major purpose is to determine "what may be."
EX-Will subjects receiving individualized instruction achieve more than the students receiving traditional reading group instruction?

EX POST FACTO RESEARCH
Similar to experimental research except investigator cannot directly manipulate independent variables.
EX-Did my students achieve less than a comparable class because they didn't have a regular teacher?

EXTERNAL CRITERION
One needs an external criterion that is known to be a measure of the variable involved and can be used to compare one's predictions. Success in college, as reflected by grade point average is a clearly defined external criterion for validating those tests that are constructed for the selection of college applicants.
EX-Number of library books read outside of class assignments is an *external criterion* of reading enjoyment.

FREQUENCY
Refers in statistics to the number of times a score is repeated or to the number of scores appearing in a given interval.
EX-Joe and Sally got 85% on the spelling test, Fred, Donna, Shirley and Bob got 80%. Frequency for 85 = 2. Frequency for 80 = 4.

FREQUENCY DISTRIBUTION
A systematic arrangement of individual measures from highest to lowest. The use of this technique merely involves making a list of the individual measures in a column, with the highest measure at the top, the next highest, second from the top, continuing down until the lowest measure is recorded at the bottom of the column.
EX-

# of words correct	# of people rec'd score frequency
10	2
7	6
5	5
3	2
1	1

GRADE EQUIVALENT
The grade for which the ability is typical.
EX-Kathy is achieving at the 4th grade level, 3rd month on the Metropolitan Achievement tests. Her grade equivalent is 4.3.

HISTORICAL RESEARCH
A procedure supplementary to observation. A process by which the historian seeks to test the truthfulness of the reports of observations made by others. Its major purpose is to tell "what was."
EX-Tracing the evaluation of the open classroom.

HYPOTHESIS
A tentative proposition suggested as a solution to a problem or as an explanation of some phenomenon. It presents in simple form a statement of the researcher's expectations relative to a relationship between variables with the problem. It is then tested in a research study.
EX-Students who attend a remedial reading clinic five hours a week will improve their scores on the Metropolitan Primary Achievement Tests significantly more than students who attend the clinic for only three hours a week.

INDEPENDENT VARIABLES
Variables that are antecedent to the dependent variable are called independent variables. This is the factor that is measurably separate and distinct from the dependent variable but may relate to the dependent variable. Many factors that may function as independent variables are discriminate aspects of the environment, such as, social class, home environment, and classroom conditions. In addition, characteristics of the individual himself such as age, sex, intelligence and motivation-may be independent variables that can be related to the dependent variable.
EX-A child's height (dependent variable) would be dependent to a certain extent upon his age (independent variable). These terms are often used even in the absence of empirical or theoretical reasons for considering one to be the antecedent and the other to be the consequence. They are used to indicate the direction of prediction from individuals' positions on the independent variable to their positions on the dependent variable. This is sometimes called the active variable. Examples of Dependent and Independent variables:
1. *Reading achievement* (D.V.) is affected by *Self-concept* (I.V.).
2. *Word knowledge* (D.V.) is dependent on *Social economic status* (I.V.).
3. *Reading achievement* (D.V.) is dependent on *Reading enjoyment* (I.V.).

INFERENTIAL STATISTICS
The process of going from the part to the whole. A population comprises all the possible cases (persons, objects or events) that constitute a known whole. A sample is a portion of a population.
EX-A representative sample of 1000 six year old children obtain a mean raw score of 48 on the WISC. It is then inferred that the "average" 6 year old will obtain a score of 48 of the WISC.

INFERRED DIMENSION
A property or quality of a phenomenon not itself observable but imput or *inferred* to a phenomenon.
EX-A child's knowledge is measured by an I.Q. test.

INTERCORRELATION
A term applied to each of the correlations among a group of tests. Usually displayed in tables showing the correlation of each test with each of the other test. They are then used to show the extent of interrelationships among a certain group of tests.
EX-If a child scores high on the reading comprehension tests in Gates-MacGinite test, then he will probably score high on the vocabulary test.

INTERVAL SCALE
Not only indicates the relative position of individuals but also provides additional information about these positions because this type of scale uses predetermined equal intervals.

Such scales do not necessarily have a true zero point. Arbitrary zero points may be used, but such points are by no means absolute. Consider intelligence tests, for example. In these tests there are zero points and it is conceivable that one's score could be zero, but zero scores in these tests do not mean zero intelligence. For this reason it is not possible to compare an intelligence test score of 75 with a score of 150 and say the latter score is twice as high as the former.
EX-Number of correct spelling words on an exam. Score on the Stanford-Binet test.

LEVEL OF SIGNIFICANCE
A statistical term used to indicate the amount of confidence in whether or not the difference between two means, two percentages or other comparable measures is statistically significant (not due to chance). Also referred to as significance of difference and statistical difference.
EX-If Suzie got a 93% on a spelling test and Bill got a 90%, is Suzie a significantly better speller, or is her better score simply due to chance?

MEASUREMENT
The assignment of a symbol, often a number, so as to characterize the status of a phenomenon relative to some dimension, usually by indicating its scale position, its rank, or its classification per this dimension.
EX-Joe got 15 out of 20 spelling words correct, or 75% of them correct. This is a measurement of correct replies. If the score he received is the fourth highest test score, it is a measurement of his rank compared to others.

MEAN
The most widely used measure of central tendency is the mean, which is popularly known as the average or *arithmetic average*. It is the sum of all the values in a distribution divided by the number of cases. In terms of a formula it is:
$X = EX/IN$ where: X = the mean
E = the sum of
X = each of the values in the distribution
N = number of cases
EX-The average or mean Reading test score -

Jo- 8
Sally - 3
Mike - 6
Tom - 7
24/4 = 6 = ave.

MEDIAN
The score or point that divides a distribution of scores into two equal groups with half of the scores falling above and half below. Used as a representative score or a measure of central tendency.
EX-Scores: 4 12 18 21 26. 18 is the center score, it is the median.

MODE
The score or measure that occurs most frequently in a distribution.
EX - 3 students got 90 on their exam.
6 students got 85 on their exam.
1 student got 84 on his/her exam.
8 students got 80 on their exam.

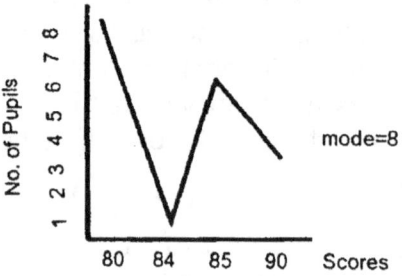

NOMINAL SCALE
The simplest type of scale and provides the lowest level of quantification of the objects to be measured. A nominal scale simply sorts objects, or classes of objects, into mutually exclusive categories. Our data will only tell us how many of the subjects belong to each groupA or how many students of a class are boys and how many are girls. Dividing individuals into such categories as smokers and non-smokers; Democrats, Republicans, and independents; elementary, junior high, and secondary; tall and short; and so on, are all examples of nominal scales.
EX-When we label the experimental units in a study as groups A, B, C, and D, or when we divide the students of a class into boys and

girls, we are using a nominal scale in each of these examples.

NORMAL CURVE
A symmetrical distribution of measures with the same number of cases at specified distances below the mean as above the mean. Its mean is the point below which exactly 50% of the cases are located. The median and the mode in such a distribution are identical values and coincide with the mean. In a normal curve, most of the cases concentrate near the mean.
EX-

NORMS
Statistics based upon a standardization group or a group that is purported to be representative of a much larger population. These norms are thus assumed to be representative of large groups.
EX-All fifth-grade children or all twelve-year-olds, grade, age percentile, and standard score norms are the most common forms.

OBSERVATION
The most widely used and usually most crude method of behavioral measurements. Involves direct perception of the dimensions of the phenomenon being measured. With appropriate attentional, perceptual, and recording aids, observation can be a highly reliable procedure.
EX-Frequency count-Phillip got out of his seat without permission six times in the fifty minute reading period. Interval count-Mary was not attending to the lesson for 40% of the thirty second intervals recorded.

OPERATIONAL DEFINITION
Ascribes meaning to a concept or construct by specifying the operations that must be performed in order to measure the concept. This type of definition is essential in research, since data must be collected in terms of observable events. When one defines a concept or construct operationally, he chooses discriminable events as indicators of the abstract concept and devises operations to obtain data relevant to the concepts. An operational definition thus refers to the operations by which an investigator may measure a concept. These are essential to research because they permit investigators to measure abstract concepts and constructs and permit a scientist to move from the level of constructs and theory to the level of observation, upon which science is based.
EX-Operationalized definition of achievement-scores obtained on the Stanford Diagnostic Achievement Test. Operationalized definition of reading enjoyment number of books read outside of class, not for assignments.

ORDINAL SCALE
The use of the ordinal scale permits the sorting of objects or classes of objects on the basis of their standing relative to each other. This scale not only categorizes but also ranks the objects on the basis of some criterion. A teacher who ranks his students on the basis of their intelligence, achievement, class participation, discipline, creativity, or any other characteristic is making use of an ordinal scale.
EX-Rank in class, percentile rank, percentiles.

POPULATION
Used in an abstract sense in measurement and statistics to indicate any given group of things, the total group in question not just part of it.
EX-All the pupils in the sixth grade in your school district is the population from which your sample (the children in your sixth grade class) is taken.

PRACTICE EFFECT
It is known that a performance of any task affects a reperformance of that task, usually in the direction of improvement. *Practice effect* is the term for the significance of such reperformance when the same test is administered to the same individual more than once.
EX-When pupils do better on a quiz the second time it is given in a week, is this because they know the material better or because they have had practice with the question.

PRETEST
Any measuring instrument (usually an achievement test) administered prior to a period of instruction, an experiment, or other circumstance of interest. As a rule pretests are used to establish the initial status of pupils so that the amount of their learning may be judged from the results of a later retest.
EX-Students are given the Metropolitan Primary Achievement test in September and again in May. The tests in September would be a pretest.

PROBABILITY
As applied to behavioral measurement, the concept that any measure or statistic is somewhat subject to chance variation. Hence it deviates from some theoretically "true" measure. Such deviation is commonly called error and its probable extent can be determined and stated mathematically. *See Level of Significance.*
EX-There is .05 or 5% chance that these scores were obtained by chance.

PRODUCT ANALYSIS
A basic procedure of educational evaluation in which the things that pupils produce in the course of instruction are appraised in appropriate ways and given scores or ratings.
EX-Compositions, outlines.

PRODUCT MOMENT FORMULA
A widely used formula for the correlation coefficient. Let Zx be the standard score for variable y. If the pairs of Zx's and Zy's for each individual are multiplied, then added for all individuals and divided by the number of cases, the result is the product moment formula for the correlation coefficient. The correlation coefficient is the mean of the set of products of standard scores for the two variables.

EX- $r = \sum \frac{(Zx\, Zy)}{n}$

Zx = Z - scores for all x
Zy = Z - scores for all y
n = number of subjects

PROFILE
An analytic graphic presentation of a pupil's scores on a test battery, scores on parts of a given test, marks in several school subjects, ratings on several personality variables, etc.
EX-

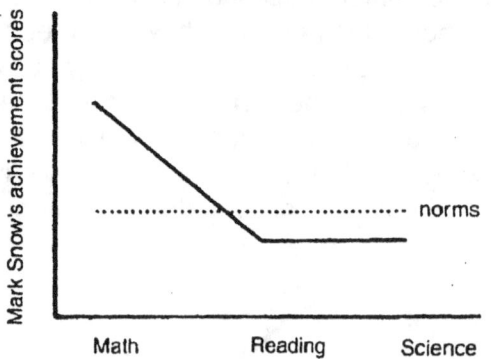

RANDOM SAMPLING
The basic characteristic of random sampling is that all members of the population have an equal and independent chance of being included in the sample. That is, for every pair of elements x and y, x's chance of being selected equals y's chance, and the selection of x in no way affects y's probability of selection.
EX-Mary, Joe and Sally are in Ms. Brown's class. She decides to choose 2 of them to do an experiment. She puts all of their names in a hat. They all have an equal chance to be chosen and if one is chosen this does not affect the chances of the others being chosen.

RANGE
The difference between the highest and lowest scores in a given distribution of scores.
EX-If the highest score in a distribution as 74 and the lowest as 30, the range would be: R = 74 - 30 = 44.

RANKING
The process of ordering the constituents of a group in terms of some dimension. Rank numbers indicate the relative position of the constituents.
EX-Scores on a reading achievement test

S	6.3	6.1	6.0	6.0	6.0	5.5	5.1
R	1	2	4	4	4	6	7.5

RATING
A direct appraisal of a dimension in terms of some descriptive scale or verbal classification scheme.
EX-Children are rated by their teacher for their disruptive behavior: 1 = very disruptive; 2 = average; 3 = quiet.

RATIO SCALE
The highest level of measurement is provdied by a ratio scale. In addition to having equal intervals, a ratio scale measures from a meaningful zero. Most physical measures have a meaningful zero. The scale used in education measurements are seldom of this level of measurement.
EX-Using a ratio scale we can say that John is 48 inches tall, Ralph is 45 inches tall, and Paul is 44 inches tall; but using an interval scale we are only able to say that John is 3 inches taller than Ralph, whp is one inch taller than Paul. Not only can we say that the difference between 60 and 90 pounds is the same as the difference between 90 pounds and 120 pounds, but we can say that 120 pounds is twice as heavy as 60 pounds. We can do this because zero weight is an actual possibility.

RAW SCORE
The first quantitative untreated result obtained in scoring a test.
EX-Bill got 98% on vocabulary test.
    Jill got 83% on vocabulary test.
    Tony got 78% on vocabulary test.

READING GRADE
A type of "norm" score derived from standardized tests that states a pupil's ability to read in terms of grade equivalents. Reading grade means the school grade whose average performance is most like that of the pupil in question. By interpolation, the reading grade be fractional. As with reading age, reading grade refers only to a given standardized test.
EX-Ann received a 6.3 on the Gates-MacGinities Test. She is performing at sixth grade, three month level of achievement.

RELIABILITY
The extent to which a measuring device is constant in measuring whatever it measures.
EX-Will Greg receive approximately the same score on the Reading Achievement test if he takes it a second time two weeks after he took it the first time?

RESEARCH PROBLEM
A question concerning the relationships existing between sets of events (variables) in education. Research is conducted in order to find answers to these questions. One of the most fruitful sources for the beginning researcher is his experience as an educational practitioner. Decisions must be made daily about the probable effects of educational experience on pupil behavior.
EX-What is the effectiveness of using verbal instructions compared to written ones?

RETEST (also called a Post-test)
A test readministered at the end of a period of instruction or other activity, the result of which is to be compared with an earlier administration of a test.
EX-A list of spelling words are given at the beginning of the week to determine which words a child needs to learn. After working on the words all week, a test is given Friday to find if the pupils learn the words. The test on Friday would be considered a retest or post-test.

RHO (Q)
The rank-difference measure of correlation. Individuals are assigned ranks with respect to each of two variables, and for each individual the difference (d) in rank is determined. These differences are squared and summed for all cases and substitution is made in the following formula.

EX- $Q(rho) = \dfrac{1 - 6 \mathrm{E} d^2}{N(N^2 - 1)}$

SAMPLE
A sample is a portion of a population.
EX-The children in Ms. Smith's class is a sample of the population of sixth grade students in that district. Reading Group A is Ms. Smith's class is a sample of her sixth grade class.

SCALING
Measurement in terms of defined and precise units that represent given amounts or degrees

of some dimension. Scale numbers indicate the number of units and hence the amount or degree of the dimension. Scale numbers refer to a fixed point of reference, usually a zero. EX-Rate your agreement with this statement on a scale of 1 to 5.

SCALING
Measurement in terms of defined and precise units that represent given amounts or degrees of some dimension. Scale numbers indicate the number of units and hence the amount or degree of the dimension. Scale numbers refer to a fixed point of reference, usually a zero. EX-Rate your agreement with this statement on a scale of 1 to 5.
1 = strongly agree
2 = agree
3 = undecided
4 = disagree
5 = strongly disagree

SCORING
A process of assigning a score (usually a number or letter symbol) to a test or pupil product. For a test, this is often done by comparing a paper with the key, marking the questions answered correctly and adding up the total.
EX-Bill got 9 words right. Score = 9.
  Judy got 15 words right. Score = 15.
  Ruth got 12 words right. Score = 12.

SELF-EVALUATION
Any of many concepts and procedures concerned with an individual observing and judging his own performance, achievement, or adjustment.
EX-Coopersmith Self-Esteem Inventory.

STANDARD DEVIATION
An index of variation in a group of mesures. It represents the square root of the mean of the squared deviations of the individual measures.

EX- $SD = \sqrt{\dfrac{\Sigma d^2}{N-1}}$

d^2 = difference between score and mean
n = number of subjects

STANDARD SCORE (z score)
A general term referring to any of a number of scores that indicate how many standard deviations a measurement is above or below the mean. It is found by determining the difference between the raw score (X) and the mean (X) and dividing by the standard deviation (S).

Ex- $Z = \dfrac{X - \bar{X}}{S}$

X = Bills score
X = Class average
X = Standard deviation: (equation needed).

STANDARDIZED TESTS
Tests, usually published, which have been preadministered to a population of known characteristics and yield scores in terms of this population. This population is selected so as to be a representative sample of the total population for which the test is designed.
EX-Stanford-Binet Intelligence Test, Metropolitan Primary Achievement Test, Ginn Reading Achievement Test.

STANINE
Any one of nine intervals on a scale of standard scores. The "stanine" (abbreviation for standard-nine) scale spans the normal curve in nine intervals of size equal to one half of a standard score. The stanine intervals have values from 1 to 9 and the middle interval, 5, extends from standard score - 1/4 to + 1/4.
EX-

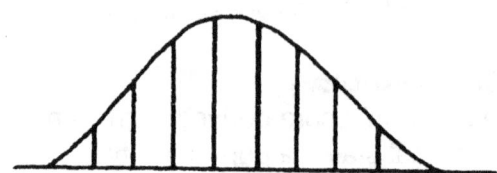

STATISTICAL PROCEDURES
Basic methods of handling quantitative information in such a way as to make that information meaningful. These procedures have two principal advantages for the researcher. First, they enable him/ her to describe and summarize his observations. Such techniques are called *descriptive statistics*. Second, they help him/her determine how reliably (s)he can infer that phenomena observed in a limited group, *a sample,* will also occur in the unobserved

larger population of concern, from which the sample was drawn. In other words, how well (s)he can employ inductive reasoning to infer that what (s)he observes in the part will be observed in the whole. For problems of this nature (s)he will need to employ *inferential statistics*.
EX-Finding the mean score-*descriptive statistics*. Finding if there is significant differences-inferential *statistics*.

STATISTIC(S)
Any derived quantity obtained from a set of raw scores or measures.
EX-N, mean, standard deviation, median, mode, quartile deviation, correlation coefficient.

TESTS
Any of a great number of procedures in which individuals respond to a common stimulation in comparable ways and which yield a measure of the individuals with respect to one or more dimensions.
EX-Achievement tests, Personality tests, Spelling tests, Performance tests, Ability tests.

VALIDATION
The process of establishing on the basis of empirical data the validity of a test, usually a standardized one, by comparing its results with one or more criteria. Typically involves, as a minimum item analysis, correlation of results with other test scores, analysis of distributions of scores, and determination of reliability.
EX-See test manual or Mental Measurement Yearbook by Buros to find out about a test validation.

VALIDITY
The extent to which an instrument measures what it is supposed to measure.
EX-A test measures a pupil's reading comprehension not size of vocabulary or general knowledge.

VARIABLE
A concept that can take on different values.
EX-It can vary within an individual from one time to another, between individuals at the same time, between the averages for groups, and so on. Social class, sex, motivation, intelligence quotient, and spelling test scores are other examples of variables. Educational researchers are interested in determining how such variables are related to each other.

VARIANCE
The mean of the squared deviation scores.

EX- $S^2 = \sum \dfrac{(X-\bar{X})^2}{N}$

$X - \bar{X}$ = difference between score and mean
N = number of subjects

www.ingramcontent.com/pod-product-compliance
Lightning Source LLC
Chambersburg PA
CBHW080322020526
44117CB00035B/2606